CRESCENT BOOKS

New York

The Fields of Summer

America's Great Ballparks
and the
Players Who Triumphed in Them

James Tackach and Joshua B. Stein

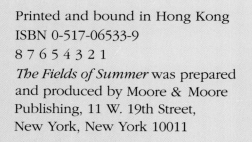

This 1992 edition was published by Crescent Books, distributed
by Outlet Book Company, Inc., a Random House Company,
225 Park Avenue South, New York, New York 10003

Printed and bound in Hong Kong
ISBN 0-517-06533-9
8 7 6 5 4 3 2 1
The Fields of Summer was prepared
and produced by Moore & Moore
Publishing, 11 W. 19th Street,
New York, New York 10011

Dedications

To George, who always took his kid brother along, including
to his first baseball game more than 30 summers ago.   *J.T.*

To my son Jeremy, whose love of sports is exceeded only by
my love for him.   *J.B.S.*

Previous pages Fenway Park, Boston, Massachusetts

These pages *Clockwise from upper left:* Old Timers's Day, Fenway Park, Boston, Massachusetts, 1987; Ebbets Field, Brooklyn,
New York; Stan Musial, St. Louis Cardinals; Detroit Tigers
Scorebook, 1971; Astrodome, Houston, Texas; Vintage glove
and ball; Ty Cobb, Detroit Tigers

Pages 10–11 Wrigley Field, Chicago, Illinois

Pages 96–97 Royals Stadium, Kansas City, Missouri

Page 160 Candlestick Park, San Francisco, California

AN M&M BOOK

Project Director & Editor Gary Fishgall

Editorial Assistants Maxine Dormer, Ben D'Amprisi, Jr.; **Copy
Editor** Judith Rudnicki

Designers Delgado Design and Marcy Stamper

Separations and Printing Regent Publishing Services Ltd.

C O N T E N T S

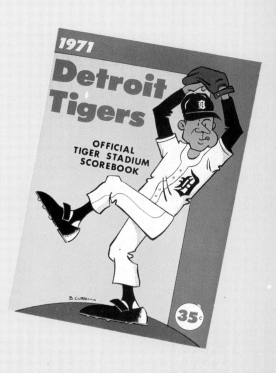

INTRODUCTION

I

N MOST PROFESSIONAL SPORTS, the contours of the playing field are rigidly defined. An American football field is 100 yards from goal line to goal line and 53 1/3 yards wide. A professional basketball court is 94 feet by 50 feet, and the baskets are exactly ten feet high. Tennis courts are 78 feet long and 36 feet wide; the height of the net and size of the serving boxes also conform to exact specifications.

But the dimensions of a professional baseball field are not so clearly stipulated. Yes, the bases must be laid 90 feet apart as Alexander Cartwright specified in his 1845 rule book, and the pitcher's mound must be exactly 60 feet, 6 inches from home plate, a distance arrived at only after considerable experimentation. But the specifications for the rest of the field—the distance from home plate to the outfield fences, the height of the barriers surrounding the playing field, the width of the territory between the foul lines and the first row of box seats—are inexact; some general guidelines are set down in the official rule book, but a great deal of latitude is allowed. The result, of course, is that baseball parks and stadiums have been created in a rich variety of shapes and sizes— from intimate street-corner fields to sprawling, domed superstructures set in a sea of parking lots. And in no sport, except perhaps golf, has the layout of the playing field had more effect on the game being played.

Before the era of steel-and-concrete stadiums, most major league ballparks were made of wood, like the Huntington Avenue Baseball Grounds, home of the Boston Red Sox from 1901 through 1911. This photo shows the crowd swarming the field after the deciding game of the 1903 World Series.

This book celebrates major league ballparks. It pays homage to 25 of the arenas that have housed America's National Pastime—some alive only in memory, others the setting for today's pennant races and World Series contests. Along the way, we'll recall some of the noteworthy events that have taken place in these arenas, events that are among the most memorable in baseball's rich history.

Although this book begins with the first steel-and-concrete stadiums of the pre-World War I era, the history of baseball stadiums winds back to the Civil War.

Baseball is a pastoral game; its first fields were open meadows and cow pastures, like Elysian Fields in Hoboken, New Jersey, the site of the first baseball game played under Cartwright's rules. During these early games, spectators spread their blankets a safe distance from the diamond and relaxed while they observed the action. No fences or grandstands enclosed the field, and a fee was rarely collected from the bystanders.

In 1862, however, William Cammeyer, a New York businessman, got the idea of turning a profit from the sport that was gaining rapid popularity in the metropolitan area. Using racetrack grandstands as his model, Cammeyer laid out a baseball field on a piece of his land in the Williamsburg section of Brooklyn and enclosed it with a wooden grandstand. He called the 1,500-seat arena Union Grounds and allowed local teams to use the field for free, while charging fans ten cents apiece to see them play. Thus, the baseball stadium was born.

After the Civil War, the sport flourished, and baseball arenas sprang up all over the East Coast. In the late 1860s, when the first professional players and teams appeared, it became even more necessary to hold games in enclosed grandstands so that revenue could be raised for the players' salaries. When the National League was formed in 1876, all of its clubs were playing in enclosed fields like the one built by Cammeyer.

Throughout the rest of the 19th century, ballparks grew in size, and conveniences like rest rooms and concession stands were added, but the arenas greatly resembled

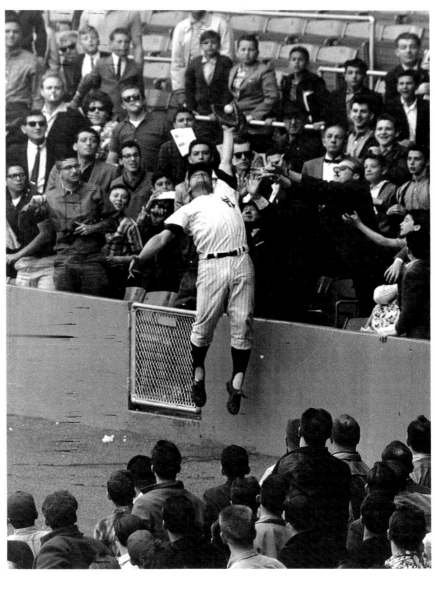

Only at the ballpark can fans get in on the action, like these patrons battling Roger Maris for a long drive in deep right field at Yankee Stadium.

the Williamsburg prototype. These early stadiums, however, had one major drawback: they were dangerously susceptible to fire. In 1894 alone, National League parks in Boston, Chicago, Baltimore, and Philadelphia were either severely damaged or completely destroyed by flames. In 1899, the home of the Louisville Colonels burned to the ground, and the city lost its franchise the next season.

It was both a fear of fire and a desire for profit that ushered in the next phase of ballpark design. Late in 1908, Ben Shibe, owner of the American League's Philadelphia Athletics, began laying plans for a new ballpark to house his team. He wanted to create an arena impressive enough to draw fans from his crosstown rivals, the Phillies. The result, Shibe Park, was baseball's first modern stadium, a 20,000-seat grandstand built entirely of concrete and steel and surrounded by a spectacular French Renaissance facade.

Shibe Park, which opened in 1909, was the envy of baseball owners around the country, and similar edifices were soon erected in Pittsburgh, Chicago, Boston, Brooklyn, New York, and Washington. The era of the wooden ballpark was over.

Though the new ballparks imitated Shibe's construction, they varied greatly in design and appearance. Because the three surviving pre-World War I parks—Fenway Park, Tiger Stadium, and Wrigley Field—have small playing dimensions that favor the hitters, we tend to assume that all older parks were of that mold. Some ballparks were indeed tiny, because they had to be shoehorned into an existing grid of city streets. But other stadiums, like Forbes Field and Griffith Stadium, built on the outskirts of Pittsburgh and Washington, D.C., respectively, were pitcher-friendly, with huge outfield lawns and distant fences. Moreover, the pre-World War I parks featured an odd collection of fences and walls, and grandstands were added in jury-rig fashion over the years to accommodate more seats. Each park had unique features; no two looked the same.

The next stage of stadium design, which began after World War II, was ushered in by the franchise shifts of the 1950s, which left Braves Field, the Polo Grounds, and beloved Ebbets Field abandoned. The new stadiums were generally larger than the ballparks left behind. More importantly, most were built with taxpayers' money (a trend begun with Cleveland Stadium in 1932), and some were built to house both baseball and football. These trends continued when, during the 1960s, it became apparent that something had to be done about the aging ballparks in Pittsburgh, Philadelphia, Cincinnati, and St. Louis. Rather than refurbish the old grounds, new parks were created in these cities.

The new stadiums were large facilities, symmetrical in shape—because they did not always have to be wedged into urban neighborhoods—and designed to accommodate two or three sports so that the taxpayers who financed them could get their money's worth. Because the stadiums were multipurpose—baseball during the week, college football on Saturday, professional football on Sunday, a soccer match on Sunday night, a rock concert on Monday—their playing surfaces were covered with no-maintenance artificial turf. Baseball purists derided the new facilities, claiming that they lacked the variety and uniqueness of their ancestors.

It is the very irregularity of the playing surfaces of the older parks that appealed to traditionalists. Fenway Park is friendly to right-handed hitters; Ebbets Field was a lefty's delight. The Polo Grounds' deep center field was a pitcher's dream, but the park's short left field porch was his nightmare. Purists maintain that a baseball stadium's irregularities reflect life's unpredictabilities: our lives are not divided into 100 evenly spaced yard markers or set in a finite server's box; the world, like the old ballparks, is unpredictable, at times unfair, at other times working in our favor.

The crowd, standing on its feet, rooting the home team on, is an integral part of the National Pastime. The female rooter in the center of this photo has a particularly good reason to cheer. Her husband, Joltin' Joe DiMaggio, has just tied Willie Keeler's record for hitting safely in 44 consecutive games.

If the traditionalists were unenthusiastic about the new modernistic ballparks, they liked the domed stadiums even less. But the Houston Astrodome, which opened in 1965, was deemed a successful experiment, so domes for baseball were erected in Seattle, Minneapolis, and Toronto as well.

In the past two years, however, lovers of the older urban parks have had reason to cheer. Preservation efforts in Detroit seem to have saved Tiger Stadium from the wrecker's ball, at least for now. Venerable Comiskey Park was lost, but its replacement, a grass-covered, baseball-only stadium a stone's throw from the old park, is not an insult to traditionalist sensibilities. And the new park opening in Baltimore in 1992, with its inner-city location, brick facade, and asymmetrical design, is a throwback to the extinct arenas of the pre-World War I era.

So the landscape of contemporary baseball continues to be adorned with a variety of playing houses—domed stadiums that feature all the engineering magic of the age, sleek superstructures designed for convenience and efficiency, and some golden old ballparks of a bygone era.

To most of us, however, a ballpark is much more than a place where baseball is played. It is a magical kingdom, a fantasy land, an escape from the humdrum world of school and office

Those of us born between 1940 and 1960 came into this world when televised games were being broadcast on a regular basis. Our television screens were small, the images black, white, and gray. There was a single camera angle most of the time—above and behind the catcher, capturing the action around home plate. If the batter made contact, another camera could zoom in showing the fielder making or muffing the play, but then it was back to the boring over-the-shoulder shots.

But then our fathers, uncles, or grandfathers took us to our first game. And the imprint of that experience remains clear even 30 or 40 years later. We can still recall the excitement of walking into the outer foyer of the stadium on a clear midsummer day, then working our way through an archway toward the box seat area.

What youngster doesn't want to take home a souvenir from his or her trip to the ballpark? This enterprising lad, however, is selling, not buying, during an April 1954 game at Baltimore's Memorial Stadium.

Seeing the field for the first time was almost a religious experience, as inspiring as entering a church or synagogue. The green of the grass, the brown of the dirt basepaths, the white of the chalk lines; vendors hawking, kids shouting, the balls hitting the leather of the gloves, the crack of the wooden bats—television had prepared us for none of this. Hot dogs and sausages scented the air, and peanut shells cracked pleasingly underfoot with every step. Television could never approximate those sensations. How long had this been going on? Our fathers knew; we were just finding out.

And the players! There was Stan Musial in his Cardinal-red accented uniform, crouching in his familiar stance, cracking a ball against an outfield fence. Ebony-faced Jackie Robinson dancing off third base, and the opposing pitcher fidgeting nervously. Mickey Mantle, broad back, hulking arms and shoulders, kneeling in the on-deck circle, squeezing his bat, and staring down the pitcher.

From that first trip to the ballpark, the game was never the same, not for any of us who have made the pilgrimage. And the love of the baseball diamond, the thrill of the experience, the sounds, the smells, the hopes, and the frustrations—all, in fact, that a ballpark conjures up—is what we hope you will recall as you read these pages and peruse these pictures.

We have chosen to highlight 25 ballparks, starting with the first modern stadiums of 1909 and concluding with the brand new parks in Chicago and Baltimore. We have tried to provide a proper mix of older arenas that will stir pleasant memories for nostalgic readers and newer parks that are the settings for the contemporary game.

So join us on a tour of these fields of summer. A box seat is waiting for you.

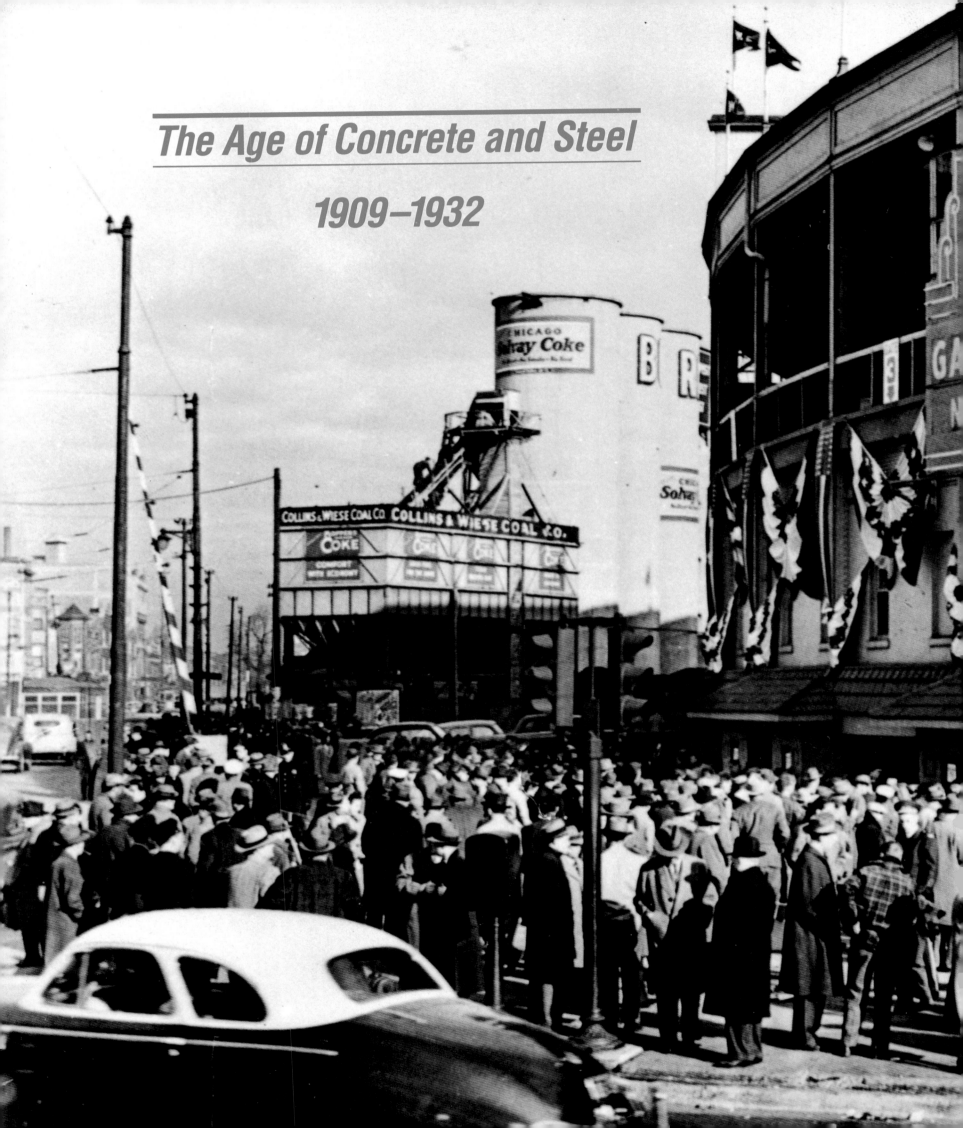

The Age of Concrete and Steel

1909–1932

The menu at this Shibe Park concession stand shows that the old ballparks featured a wide variety of items at affordable prices.

During World War II, Shibe Park allowed free entry to all military personnel. The American soldiers seen here were in line for a Phillies-Giants game in the spring of 1942.

S H I B E PARK

Philadelphia, Pennsylvania

1909–1970

SHIBE PARK, the first baseball arena built entirely with steel and concrete, was arguably the most magnificent structure ever to house the National Pastime. Built in 1908 on 5 3/4 acres of North Philadelphia farmland, Shibe Park (later Connie Mack Stadium) was revolutionary in construction and design. The other baseball arenas of the day were wooden edifices that differed little from the ballparks of the post-Civil War era. When Shibe opened on April 12, 1909, these old arenas were at once doomed, and the modern era of stadium construction had begun.

The park was the creation of Ben Shibe, the controlling owner of the Philadelphia Athletics, and Connie Mack, his team's innovative manager. Prior to the park's opening, the A's played in Columbia Park, a tiny, single-deck, wooden grandstand built for the club when it joined the newly formed American League in 1901. Shibe and Mack wanted a large and impressive arena, one that could lure fans from their crosstown rivals, the National League's Phillies. The Phils' home park was the Baker Bowl, which was at that time baseball's most up-to-date stadium, featuring partial concrete-and-steel construction and the first cantilevered

Shibe Park served as a home for the Philadelphia Athletics from its opening in 1909 until the team's departure for Kansas City in 1954. It also hosted the Philadelphia Phillies from 1938 through 1970.

Shibe Park was named for Ben Shibe, the manufacturer who owned the Athletics. The revolutionary ballpark was the creation of Shibe and Connie Mack, the team's innovative manager.

grandstand in the country.

Shibe and Mack's new ballpark was indeed an eye-opener. It held 20,000 seats in a single-deck pavilion that wrapped around home plate and uncovered bleachers that extended up the foul lines, and an additional 10,000 fans could be admitted to stand in a roped-off area in deep center field. More impressive than the park's interior, however, was its external French Renaissance facade. Shibe's brick outer walls were accented with terra cotta trim and arched windows, and its main gate at 21st Street and Lehigh Avenue featured a splendid Beaux-Arts tower that housed the club's executive offices. From the street, Shibe Park looked more like a Renaissance cathedral than a baseball stadium. More than 30,000 fans crammed into the park on opening day, and thousands were turned away, many of whom gladly surrendered their ticket money to the neighborhood entrepreneurs who sold standing room on the rooftops of apartment buildings overlooking the field.

Shibe's field was enormous. The park had been built on the outskirts of town, so existing buildings did not restrict the dimensions of the outfield lawn. Originally, the left field fence was 378 feet from home plate, and the fence in right field was set at 340 feet. The center field wall—515 feet from the batter's box—was unreachable in this dead-ball era; and over the years, wise Philadelphia managers assigned a speedster to cover the vast center field territory. Richie Ashburn, who played for the Phillies from 1948 through 1959, probably did it best.

This $6.60 ticket afforded a fan a box seat for game four of the 1929 World Series between the Philadelphia Athletics and the Chicago Cubs.

Imitation is said to be the sincerest form of flattery and after Shibe Park's debut, other baseball magnates followed Ben Shibe's lead. During the next five years, concrete-and-steel stadiums opened in Pittsburgh, St. Louis, Brooklyn, Chicago, Boston, Washington, and New York. The era of the wooden major league ballpark had come to an end.

So pervasive, in fact, was Shibe's influence, that the park itself soon became obsolete, at least as far as size was concerned. Baseball enjoyed a new wave of popularity during the 1920s, as fans around the country jammed stadiums to see Babe Ruth, Rogers Hornsby, and other future Hall of Famers perform their magnificent feats. Accordingly, Shibe Park was enlarged. A second deck was erected atop the grandstand in 1925, and bleacher seats were also added. The left field bleachers were eventually doubled-decked, and a mezzanine was built in 1929, bringing the park's capacity to almost 35,000 (with an additional 5,000 standees shoehorned in for big games). As part of these renovations, the outfield fences were pushed closer to home plate, helping Jimmy Foxx win three home run titles during his Philadelphia seasons. But the ease of hitting home runs did not last. In 1934, the 12-foot right field fence was replaced by a 50-foot corrugated metal barrier whose purpose was to prevent fans from watching games from the rooftops of the apartment buildings that overlooked the park.

On July 4, 1938, the Phillies finally abandoned the crumbling Baker Bowl and joined the Athletics in Shibe. Thus, for the next 16 seasons, the park had two tenants. The National Football League's Philadelphia Eagles joined them in 1940, playing at Shibe Park until 1958.

Any baseball stadium with the longevity of Shibe Park is bound to have a rich and exciting history, and that is most certainly the case here. Connie Mack—who would manage the A's for 50 seasons—entered Shibe Park with a team that would win the World Series in 1910, 1911, and 1913. But after the pennant-winning 1914 season, Mack, for financial reasons, sold his best players, and the A's spent the next seven seasons in the American League basement. He built another great team in the late 1920s and won three straight pennants (1929–1931) and two World Series (1929 and 1930) at a time when the Yankees were said to be unbeatable. In the fourth game of the 1929 Series, at Shibe Park, the A's created the greatest rally in World Series history, overcoming an 8-0 Cub lead with 10 seventh-inning runs. But in the 1930s, Mack, reeling from the Great Depression, sold Al Simmons, Jimmy Foxx, Mickey Cochrane, Lefty Grove, and other mainstays of that club. The A's spent most of the next 20 seasons in the second division and finally departed for Kansas City after the 1954 season.

"Program here!" This one is for the 1911 World Series between the Philadelphia Athletics and the New York Giants.

Al Simmons, a future Hall of Famer, played for the Athletics when they won American League pennants in 1929, 1930, and 1931. But he, along with other mainstays of the club, was sold by manager Connie Mack, who was reeling from the Great Depression.

The great Jimmy Foxx, shown crossing home plate in game one of the 1930 World Series, played for the Athletics from 1925 through 1935.

The Athletics' roommates, the Phillies, did not fare much better. They finished last in seven of their first eight seasons at Shibe Park. In 1950, their young team, nicknamed "the Whiz Kids," surprised everyone by winning the National League flag, but the Yanks swept them four straight in the World Series. Seven mediocre seasons followed, and in 1958, the Phils fell into last place, where they stayed for four more summers.

For many of Shibe Park's 62 seasons, the local fans tasted bitter disappointment. But no year was more frustrating than 1964, when the Phillies, under Gene Mauch, blew a six-game lead with two weeks left. Mauch's charges lost 10 straight games, allowing the Cardinals, the Reds, and the Giants to get back in the race. The Cards won the flag on the season's final day.

By that time, Shibe Park—renamed Connie Mack Stadium—was deteriorating badly, and its surroundings, once a working-class Irish neighborhood, had become an urban wasteland. Veterans Stadium was built across town, and the Phillies occupied it when the 1971 season opened. Fire damaged the old park that August, and it was finally razed in June 1976. Today, where baseball's most impressive arena once stood, there sits only a vacant lot.

Connie Mack: Baseball's Most Enduring Manager

Cornelius Alexander McGillicuddy was born in 1862, while his father's Massachusetts regiment was fighting the Civil War. As a young man, he worked in a shoe factory until 1886, when he signed a baseball contract with the National League's Washington Statesmen. After 11 modest big league seasons—he had a .245 lifetime average—the 31-year-old Mack, whose name had been shortened by a sportswriter to fit in a box score, was asked to manage the Pittsburgh Pirates. He had only limited success in Steeltown and was fired after the 1896 season.

But in 1900, he joined Ban Johnson in the effort to start a new baseball league, recruiting Ben Shibe to sponsor the Philadelphia entry in the new American League and agreeing to serve as Shibe's manager.

Mack worked not in baseball togs but in a suit and tie. Tall and gaunt, he was easy to spot in the Athletics' dugout, holding a scorecard and gesturing toward his fielders to get them positioned correctly.

He managed the Athletics for 50 seasons, eventually becoming the team's owner as well. Twice he sold his best players for financial reasons—in 1914 when he feared that his stars would join the newly formed Federal League and again in the 1930s when Depression losses forced him to break up the great team that had dethroned the Yankees as World Champions.

At age 87, Mack was still managing. He retired in 1950 and died six years later. Today, when baseball managers are hired and fired with stunning frequency, it is hard to imagine a field boss with the longevity of Connie Mack.

Gene Mauch, who managed the Phillies from 1960 until 1968, was at the helm during the famous "Phillies Phold" of 1964.

Shibe Park's huge center field meadow required a speedy center fielder, like Richie Ashburn, who played for the Phillies from 1948 through 1959.

The old Forbes Field scoreboard, shown here in a 1949 photograph, provided inning-by-inning scores of all of the games being played around both leagues.

Paul and Lloyd Waner— "Big Poison" and "Little Poison"—played in the same Pirate outfield from 1927 through 1940.

F RBES
FIELD
Pittsburgh, Pennsylvania

Forbes Field was the home of the Pittsburgh Pirates from 1909 through 1970 and the Homestead Grays of the Negro League from 1939 through 1948.

N APRIL 1909, as the Philadelphia Athletics were playing their first games in beautiful, new Shibe Park, workers were doing double shifts to complete another state-of-the-art stadium in another part of Pennsylvania. The previous fall, Barney Dreyfuss, owner of the Pittsburgh Pirates, had decided to replace Exposition Park, his team's home for almost 20 years, with a big new ball field, one that would be the talk of the baseball world. Exposition Park was a rickety, wooden firetrap that flooded badly during rainy weather, and Dreyfuss determined that his new stadium would be a sturdy structure that would stand for many seasons.

For his new park, Dreyfuss purchased a tract of land about three miles from downtown Pittsburgh. Some thought him foolish for choosing a site so far from the center of town, but Dreyfuss needed plenty of room. Moreover, he knew that his new stadium would be easily reachable by trolley car and that fans and players would be more comfortable if they were far away from the smog of the downtown mills. On January 1, 1909, an existing ravine was filled on the site Dreyfuss had selected, and the ground was leveled for the

Third baseman Pie Traynor played his entire 17-year career (1920–1937) with the Pirates and retired with a lifetime batting average of .320.

Roberto Clemente: Tailored for Forbes Field

Few of today's baseball fans remember seeing Honus Wagner or Pie Traynor spray their line drives around Forbes Field's monstrous outfield lawn. Patrons of the game who grew up in the 1950s and 1960s, however, will never forget the sweet swing of Roberto Clemente. A native of Puerto Rico who was originally signed by the Brooklyn Dodgers, Clemente reached the big leagues as a Pittsburgh Pirate in 1955.

Realizing that Forbes Field was unfriendly to home run hitters, Clemente tailored his swing to take full advantage of the park's dimensions. He developed a smooth line drive stroke that produced modest home run totals—240 in 18 major league seasons—but helped him win four National League batting titles and achieve a .317 lifetime average. He also played Forbes Field's enormous outfield with consummate skill, winning a dozen Gold Gloves for fielding excellence. In 1966, when he batted .317 with a career-high of 29 homers and 119 RBIs, he was voted his league's Most Valuable Player Award. But his greatest achievements came in the 1971 World Series, when he led the Pirates to their upset victory by pounding the Orioles' pitchers for a .414 average.

On the last day of the 1972 season, Clemente struck his 3,000th career hit, thereby achieving a mark matched by only 10 other players at that time. Three months later, he died in a plane crash while participating in a mercy mission to provide relief to the victims of a Nicaraguan earthquake. Baseball lost a superstar, and humankind lost a very special individual. The following summer, Clemente was posthumously inducted into the Baseball Hall of Fame.

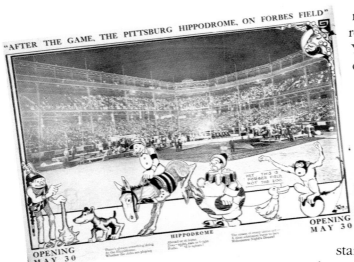

"AFTER THE GAME, THE PITTSBURG HIPPODROME, ON FORBES FIELD"

Throughout their history ballparks have been used for events other than baseball. This cartoon advertises a post-game circus to be held at Forbes Field.

new field. Construction on the stadium began two months later, under the direction of Charles W. Leavitt, a racetrack architect who had designed New York's Belmont Park, and Forbes Field—named after the British general who captured Fort Duquesne during the French and Indian War—opened on June 30. The ballpark had been built in just four months.

The Pirates' new stadium was the most magnificent ballpark in the country. Like Shibe Park, it was built with concrete and steel, yet its 25,000-seat grandstand was even larger than Shibe's. The main grandstand, which extended from the left field line around home plate and up the right field line, consisted of two levels—a lower tier with a promenade and an upper deck topped with rooftop boxes. Bleachers were set in left and center fields, behind a 12-foot wooden barrier (later replaced by an ivy-covered brick wall). Schenley Park, a public park, lay adjacent to Forbes Field's right field wall, so no stands could be erected in that area. Under the grandstand behind home plate were clubhouses for the players and the umpires. The stadium was also large enough to hold the team's offices. All the equipment in use—the field tarpaulin, the watering system, the turnstiles—was thoroughly modern.

On opening day, the new park was jammed with 30,338 excited fans who rooted for the hometown club. Perhaps spirited by their new stadium and by the huge crowds that came to see it, the Pirates won the 1909 National League pennant, then whipped the Detroit Tigers in the World Series. That Pirate team was led by Honus Wagner, the great shortstop and future Hall of Famer. On his way to Cooperstown, Wagner won eight National League batting titles and garnered 3,418 hits.

The playing surface at Forbes Field, like those in the old, wooden ballparks, was enormous—360 feet in left field, 442 feet in center field, and 376 feet in right—but tailor-made for a hitter like Wagner, who hit few home runs but whose stinging line drives often found the wide gaps between the outfielders. In 1920, three years after Wagner retired, another future Hall of Fame infielder, Pie Traynor, began spraying his line drives around Forbes Field. He led the Pirates to National League pennants in 1925 and 1927. During the 1930s, Forbes Field patrons cheered Paul and Lloyd Waner—"Big Poison" and "Little Poison." Neither hit for power, but Paul won three batting titles, and his younger brother batted more than .300 10 times during his 14 seasons with the Pirates. Both have plaques in Cooperstown. Fans of more recent vintage undoubtedly remember another Pirate hitter in the Wagner-Traynor-Waner mold—the great Roberto Clemente.

Over the years, adjustments to the Forbes Field playing surface have made the park more conducive to home runs. Double-deck stands were added in right field in

Hall of Famer Honus Wagner inspects the bats that he used to bang out 3,418 hits in his 21-year career. He played for Pittsburgh from 1900 through 1917.

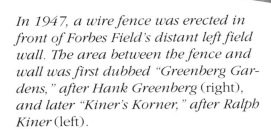

1925, reducing the distance from home plate to the right field wall by 76 feet (and providing several thousand extra seats). During the 1940s, when the Homestead Grays of the Negro National League used Forbes Field, many blasts off the bat of the great Josh Gibson found the outfield seats. In 1947, after the Pirates had acquired the Tigers' right-handed slugger, Hank Greenberg, a wire fence was placed in front of the left field wall, reducing the home run distance there by 30 feet. The untended area between the permanent wall and the new left field fence was aptly dubbed "Greenberg Gardens." Hank played in Pittsburgh only one season before retiring, but another Pirate long-baller, Ralph Kiner, was already on the scene. He led the National League in homers for seven seasons (1946–1952), and Greenberg Gardens soon became known as "Kiner's Korner."

It is ironic, given the difficulty of knocking the ball out of Forbes Field, that many of the park's most noteworthy events involve home runs. On May 25, 1935, for example, an aging and overweight Babe Ruth, playing for the Boston Braves, smacked three homers here. The last blast, the first shot ever to clear the

In 1947, a wire fence was erected in front of Forbes Field's distant left field wall. The area between the fence and wall was first dubbed "Greenberg Gardens," after Hank Greenberg (right), and later "Kiner's Korner," after Ralph Kiner (left).

The best remembered event in Forbes Field's history is Bill Mazeroski's ninth-inning homer in the seventh game of the 1960 World Series. He is shown here crossing the plate as players and fans rush to congratulate him. A ticket for the game is seen above.

(Above) *Fans rip souvenirs from the scoreboard after the final game at Forbes Field on June 28, 1970.*

Today the land once occupied by Forbes Field is part of the University of Pittsburgh. Called Forbes Quadrangle, it includes the old ballpark's home plate and a section of the center field wall.

right field roof, was Babe's 714th and last home run; he retired a week later.

But the best remembered Forbes Field highlight occurred during the 1960 World Series. In the ninth inning of the wild seventh game, with the score tied 9-9, Bill Mazeroski, the Pirates' plucky second baseman, smacked the second pitch by the Yankees' Ralph Terry over the ivy-covered left field wall. Mazeroski circled the bases, and the Pirates had their first World Championship in 35 years.

By the late 1960s, Forbes Field had fallen into disrepair, and the Pirates decided to build a new stadium. The final game at the venerable park was played on June 28, 1970. Thereafter, the Pirates went on a two-week road trip and then moved into Three Rivers Stadium. Meanwhile, the University of Pittsburgh acquired the land on which Forbes Field stood. To preserve a piece of the old park, the university left home plate in its exact location, encased in glass. It now sits in Forbes Quadrangle, a large classroom and office building. The place where the park's left field wall had stood is also marked by a plaque and a path of red bricks, and a small section of the center field wall still remains outside the Quadrangle building. These Forbes Field mementos remind contemporary students that to baseball fans they are treading sacred ground.

A dollar was all it took to get into the bleachers at Sportsman's Park for game six of the 1931 World Series—which the home team lost by a score of 8-1.

This scorecard is from the 1930 World Series, won by the Philadelphia Athletics four games to two.

(Below) Ol' number 1/8, Eddie Gaedel, walks in his first and last at bat, a brilliant publicity stunt engineered by the Browns' innovative president, Bill Veeck, on August 31, 1951.

SPORTSMAN'S
PARK
St. Louis, Missouri

1909–1966

Nestled cozily into its St. Louis neighborhood, Sportsman's Park was home to the Browns or the Cardinals or both from 1909 to 1966, though baseball had been played on the grounds since the 1860s.

SPORTSMAN'S PARK was the home of hype and heroics, a perfect blend of the best and worst that a ballpark could be. But whatever else it was, it was always fun; one simply never knew from one moment to the next what oddity would emerge to amaze.

The heroics will come later; first the hype. In deference to team owner August Busch, who was also the head of Anheuser-Busch, the manufacturers of Budweiser beer, left field once featured a neon Budweiser eagle that would flap its wings and "fly" from one end of the scoreboard to the other in celebration of each Cardinal home run. In those less cancer-conscious years, a huge advertisement for Philip Morris cigarettes, featuring the famous miniature bellhop, chirped out in a recorded voice, "Call for Philip Morris." In the 1930s, fans who came to the park early or on off days could see a goat wandering about in the outfield assisting the groundskeepers as it chewed its lunch.

The history of Sportsman's Park's anything-goes atmosphere dates back to the 1890s, when Chris Von der Ahe owned the St. Louis Browns, the American Association team that played there. (He also owned the adjacent bar.) Von der Ahe stimulated income (if not interest in the

Hall of Famer Stan "the Man" Musial demonstrates his classic crouched stance. He played for the Cards exclusively from 1941 to 1963, appearing in four World Series and winning five National League batting championships.

OFFICIAL souvenir PROGRAM
ST. LOUIS vs. DETROIT
for the Championship of the World
SPORTSMAN'S PARK ~ 1934

FIFTH GAME

(1)

(3)

CARDINALS

TIGERS

SPIRIT OF ST. LOUIS

abysmal Browns) by using his ballpark year-round as an amusement grounds and racetrack. Once, as a promotion during the baseball season, he had Buffalo Bill Cody put on one of his celebrated traveling Wild West shows there, with Sitting Bull as a featured attraction.

Is it any wonder that 60 years later, on August 19, 1951, a man who would make even Von der Ahe look like a promotional piker staged what some consider the greatest (others say the worst) publicity stunt in the history of baseball? Bill Veeck was the Browns' president at the time. The team's brief, wartime-years glory had since vanished, as had the fans, so Veeck promised to do something spectacular on the night in question. St. Louisans, used to Veeck's bizarre antics, turned up in droves to see exactly what the old huckster had in mind. In fact, when he made the boast, Veeck had nothing in mind, but almost at the last moment, he hit

The 1944 World Series: St. Louis vs. St. Louis

Between 1921 and 1956, New York City enjoyed 13 crosstown World Series. By contrast, St. Louis, which had hosted American and National League teams for a half century, found its entries meeting in the October Classic only once—in 1944.

That year, baseball was in sharp competition with the Selective Service System for physically healthy young men. Stars like Hank Greenberg, Bob Feller, Ted Williams, and Pee Wee Reese were off fighting the war, while the too young, the too old, and the 4F were left behind to keep the home fires burning and the home runs coming. Given the paucity of talent around the league, it is not surprising that for the the first (and last) time in the team's existence, the lackluster Browns captured the American League title, finishing just one game ahead of the Detroit Tigers.

The Cards had had an easy road to the championship. Led by Stan Musial, they finished 14½ games in front of second-place Pittsburgh, even after losing 15 of 20 games during one September cold streak.

Nobody gave the Browns much of a chance to win this "streetcar series," all of whose games would be played in Sportsman's Park. But the "visiting" Browns won the first game 2-1 and might have kept their streak going if not for a single awful play in game two.

In the third inning of that second contest, Cardinal pitcher Max Lanier bunted to move a runner along. Browns' pitcher Nels Potter and third baseman Mark Christman looked dumbly at each other as the ball

Browns' pitcher Jack Kramer (19) is congratulated by catcher "Red" Hayworth and third baseman Mark Christman after defeating the Cardinals in game three of the 1944 World Series by a 6-2 score.

rolled between them. Potter finally picked up the sphere, fumbled it, and then heaved it toward first base, which second baseman Don Gutteridge was covering. The throw eluded Gutteridge, and the ball caromed off the wall into right field. Right fielder Chet Laabs let the ball ricochet off the barrier and roll between his legs. He retrieved it, fumbled it, then threw it wildly toward second base. The Browns lost the game by a run in extra innings.

In game three, the Browns came roaring back, defeating the Cards by a score of 6-2. That put the Browns ahead two games to one, but the Redbirds immediately straightened out and won the next three games to cop the title. It was the last time that any ballpark played host to all of the games in the Fall Classic.

(Opposite, above) *Jubilant Gashouse Gang Cardinals celebrate copping the National League flag on the last day of the 1934 season. Back row (left to right): Joe Medwick, Bill Hallahan, coach Buzzy Wares, and Jesse Elaines. Front row: Jim Mooney, Tex Carleton, coach Mike Gonzales, Frankie Frisch, and Dizzy Dean.*

(Opposite, below) *This program is a souvenir of the 1934 World Series, when the Gashouse Gang defeated the Tigers in seven games.*

upon a true inspiration—Eddie Gaedel, all 3'7" of him. With orders not to swing at anything, Gaedel stood at the plate, bat in hand, his diminutive stature dramatically reducing the strike zone. Naturally, he drew a walk. Proudly, Gaedel, the number 1/8 on his jersey, took first base and, in the process, earned an immortal place in baseball lore for himself and his promoter.

The Cardinals' "Gashouse Gang" of the 1930s (particularly the 1934 version) provides a bridge between the hype and the heroics. These guys were zany but they knew how to play ball. With "Dizzy" and "Daffy" Dean on the mound, "Pepper" Martin at third, Leo "the Lip" Durocher at short, Frankie "the Fordham Flash" Frisch on second, Jim "the Ripper" Collins at first, and "Ducky" Medwick and company patrolling the outfield, these Cards were the most colorful and successful National League team until the pre-1958 Dodgers. They won pennants in 1930, 1931, and 1934, the last two resulting in World Series victories for Sportsman's Park fans.

As for pure heroics, perhaps the names Stan Musial, Bob Gibson, Lou Brock, and Curt Flood will stir some memories. They played all or substantial parts of their careers in Sportsman's Park, their aggregate talent significantly helping carry the Cardinals to more league pennants and World Series appearances than any other franchise except the New York Yankees.

Much of the Cardinals' success took place in a rather ordinary, classic-style, concrete-and-steel stadium, built as a single-deck grandstand for the 1909 season and expanded piecemeal during the next 20 years to seat 30,500 paying customers. Left field was 351 feet from home plate, and left center was 379 feet. Straightaway center was 422 feet, though there was a 426-foot marker. Right center was 354 feet, and along the right field foul line the wall was 310 feet from the plate. The outfield wall guarded single-deck bleachers.

Perhaps the most distinguishing feature of the park is that baseball was played on its grounds longer than at any other site. Even during the 1860s, when the field at Dodier Street and Spring Avenue was still an open lot, the sounds of bat-cracking-ball could be heard. To facilitate the implementation of an admission fee, management erected enclosed stands in 1871. The Brown Stockings of the National Association (and later of the National League) played there from 1875 through 1877. The American Association Browns played at Sportsman's Park from 1882 to 1891. The American League Browns arrived in 1902 and stayed until their departure for Baltimore in 1954, and the National League Cardinals were tenants from 1920 until they left for their new stadium early in the 1966 season. So for almost a hundred years, major league baseball was played on

St. Louisans went wild when the Cardinals won the seventh game of the 1964 World Series against the New York Yankees. The team had not been in the Fall Classic since 1946.

The beverage that shortstop Dick Groat and pitcher Bob Gibson shared after winning the 1964 World Series was not beer, but team owner Gussie Busch probably did not mind.

This is how the area that encompassed Sportsman's Park looks today. Many old ballparks have become apartment complexes, but the land on which the venerable St. Louis stadium once stood is still a park.

the diamond housed in Sportsman's Park.

The two teams who shared the field for most of its history, the Browns and the Cards, did not share in its glory. The Browns were usually cellar dwellers, except during World War II when talent was at a premium and the Browns won their only pennant. They lost the World Series to their park-mates, the mighty Cardinals, who followed their successes during the 1930s with National League pennants in 1942, 1943, and 1944. The futility of the American Leaguers was reflected in their dismal attendance. The Browns drew a club-record 712,918 fans in 1922, the year the team finished in second place and collectively won the Triple Crown: George Sisler batted a phenomenal .420, and Ken Williams copped the home run title with 39 and the RBI trophy with 155. Their low point came in 1935 with a total of only 80,922 patrons echoing in the park, barely more than 1,000 customers per game. The Cards, on the other hand, once drew 1,430,676 fans in a season (1949), while their low was a Depression-restricted 256,171 in 1933. No wonder the Browns left town while the Cardinals have remained in St. Louis, albeit in a different park, until the present day.

Sportsman's Park was associated with Jim Crow seating well into the 1940s. It is ironic, therefore, that the last home run hit in the park was belted by Willie Mays. It came in the old field's final game on May 8, 1966. Today the Herbert Hoover Boys' Club and an adjoining baseball diamond sit on the field that hosted major league baseball for nearly a century.

(Right) *Charles Comiskey became a team owner in 1894, after retiring from baseball as a player–manager. He moved his team from Sioux City, Iowa, to St. Paul, Minnesota, and then, in 1901, to his native Chicago.*

(Far right) *A hot dog vendor feeds Comiskey Park's hungry multitudes.*

This Chisox fan arriving at old Comiskey Park hopes that the hometowners will have a prosperous 1915 season. The Sox finished third.

C O M I S K E Y PARK

Chicago, Illinois

Comiskey Park was designed by Zachary Taylor Davis, the Chicago architect who would later design Wrigley Field. The venerable ballpark hosted Chicago White Sox games from 1910 through 1990.

O **N APRIL 18, 1991,** Chicago's baseball fans celebrated the opening of a new Comiskey Park on the city's South Side. Only six months earlier, however, they had mourned the loss of the first Comiskey Park, the old stadium that had served the White Sox since 1910.

Old Comiskey was conceived with the grandest of plans. In the winter of 1909, Charles Comiskey, the Chisox owner, decided to move his team from South Side Park to a new, modern facility. The previous summer, he had visited Pennsylvania's Shibe Park and Forbes Field, and he was determined to build a stadium even grander than those magnificent edifices. He hired Zachary Taylor Davis, the Chicago architect who would later design Wrigley Field, to plan a suitable stadium on a piece of land that he had purchased between West 34th and 35th Streets on the South Side. The park's green cornerstone was laid on St. Patrick's Day, and the new ballpark with its 32,000 seats was ready for baseball on July 1, 1910.

Like Shibe Park and Forbes Field, Comiskey Park was built with concrete and steel. A double-deck grandstand wrapped around home plate and up the base lines, and a single tier of wooden bleachers was placed behind the

Hall of Famer Luke Appling played shortstop for the White Sox from 1930 through 1950 and retired with a .310 lifetime batting average.

In this rare photo from game one of the 1919 World Series, Chick Gandil, one of the Chicago "Black Sox," is put out at second base. A ticket for the fourth game of the Series is at left.

The 1919 World Series: the Black Sox Scandal

Some say that old Comiskey Park was forever cursed by the events of October 1919, when eight members of the Chicago White Sox—Eddie Cicotte, Lefty Williams, Swede Risberg, Chick Gandil, Buck Weaver, Happy Felsch, Fred McMullin, and Joe Jackson—allegedly conspired with gamblers to throw the World Series.

Few suspected that a fix was in during the Series. Most fans simply thought that Williams was having a run of bad luck when the 23-game winner dropped all three of his World Series starts, or that Cicotte just lost his concentration when his two throwing errors in game four handed the Reds a 2-0 victory. After all, Shoeless Joe Jackson batted .375 in the Series, and Weaver hit .324. And the Sox won three of the eight games in the best-of-nine format.

The scandal broke the following September. In June 1921, a conspiracy trial began in Chicago with all eight "Black Sox" as defendants. But a series of highly unusual circumstances led to their acquittal. Signed confessions by Williams, Cicotte, and Jackson had mysteriously vanished before they could be entered into the record as evidence, and grand jury records also disappeared. The confessions were withdrawn, and the jury delivered a not guilty verdict. But the case was not closed. Judge Kenesaw Mountain Landis, the newly installed Commissioner of Baseball, summarily banned all eight players for life.

Today, some maintain that Jackson and one or two of the others might not have participated fully in the fix. Many argue that Shoeless Joe, whose lifetime average was .356, belongs in the Hall of Fame despite the scandal. But Judge Landis' word was law. None of the Black Sox played a major league game after 1920—and the White Sox went 20 years without a pennant.

A fan needed only a dime to buy this 1933 Comiskey Park scorecard.

outfield walls. The stadium was supposed to get a majestic Roman facade—in deference to Comiskey, who was nicknamed "the Old Roman"—but funds ran short, so a simple brick facing was placed around the grandstand. Arched windows were set in the facade, giving the stadium something of a classical appearance.

The land on which Comiskey Park sat had once been a massive garbage dump, so space constraints that dictated the quirky shapes of stadiums like Ebbets Field and Fenway Park were not a factor in the design of Comiskey. As a result, the playing field was symmetrical and very large—362 feet down the foul lines and 420 feet to dead center field. The Chisox ace pitcher "Big Ed" Walsh was a member of the committee that helped design the stadium, and he probably had some input into the decision to build the outfield walls far from home plate.

Though Comiskey Park was conceived as the grandest athletic arena in the world, it was never very pretty. For some reason, the right field grandstand was built higher than the one in left, giving the stadium a lopsided look. Moreover, expansions and alterations over the years made the park an architectural hodgepodge. The wooden bleachers were replaced by a two-tiered outfield grandstand in 1927, giving the park an extra 20,000 seats but closing it in and making it appear tomblike to some. Not even the coat of bright white paint that Bill Veeck, the maverick Chisox owner, applied in 1959 could prevent the exterior of the stadium from resembling a turn-of-the-century factory. Veeck's most noteworthy addition—a massive center field scoreboard that exploded with whistle, bells, and fireworks whenever a hometown player homered—stuck out awkwardly above the stadium's rooftop, destroying any sense of symmetry.

The activities on the field were not always pretty either. During their first five Comiskey Park seasons, the Sox finished no higher than fourth place. They won an American League pennant and a World Series in 1917 with a team of singles hitters and won another pennant in 1919, but eight members of that club were accused of throwing the World Series. Though the eight players—including the great "Shoeless Joe" Jackson—were acquitted in court, Baseball Commissioner Kenesaw Mountain Landis banned them from baseball for life. Perhaps as punishment from the baseball gods, the Chisox did not reach the World Series for another 40 years, and that appearance resulted in a loss. Comiskey Park, however, did host the first official major league All-Star Game in 1933, an event punctuated by a Babe Ruth two-run homer.

These are the American Leaguers chosen to play in the first official major league All-Star Game, held at Comiskey Park on July 6, 1933. Babe Ruth (fourth from the left in the back row, next to Lou Gehrig) homered to spark his team to a 4-2 victory.

Indeed many of Comiskey Park's "highlights" are not among baseball's greatest moments, although they have been recorded in the sport's rich folklore. One day, for example, the Sox future Hall of Fame shortstop, Luke Appling, caught his cleats on some object while going for a ground ball. It turned out to be a blue and white coffee

pot, a relic from the days when Comiskey's infield was a dump. In one game in 1960, the visiting New York Yankees lit sparklers after a Yankee homer to protest the Chisox policy of setting off the exploding scoreboard only after a hometown home run.

Bill Veeck, the White Sox owner from 1959 to 1961 and again from 1976 through 1980, was the instigator of many of the park's most memorable moments. On May 26, 1959, a helicopter landed on the infield between innings of a game against the Indians, and four midgets dressed as Martians emerged to salute Luis Aparicio and Nellie Fox, the Chisox talented but tiny keystone combo. On July 12, 1979, Veeck held a Disco Demolition Night. Patrons were asked to bring disco records to the park and turn them in for destruction between the games of a doubleheader. But fans began using the records as frisbees. Eventually thousands of spectators stormed the field and tore up the turf, forcing the Chisox to forfeit the second game of the doubleheader.

No, the park was not pretty, and the baseball played in it was rarely a thing of beauty. Nonetheless, many Chicagoans loved this park. Its eclectic design perfectly complemented the area's rough-and-tumble ethnic neighborhoods that sprung up as Irish, Italian, and Eastern European immigrants streamed into Chicago to work in the nearby stockyards and slaughterhouses. The stadium's factory decor meshed with the housing projects built for southern African-Americans who took the Illinois Central Railroad north and settled in Chicago. Wrigley Field, on Chicago's North Side, is more picturesque—an Ivy League ball yard filled with college kids and young professionals.

Bill Veeck, twice owner of the Chisox, installed the huge, exploding scoreboard at the stadium in 1960. He was also the instigator of many of the park's most memorable publicity gimmicks.

So great was the demand for tickets to see the Beatles during their 1965 American tour that ballparks were the only arenas big enough to hold the crowds. Here the lads from Liverpool are seen in their Comiskey Park engagement.

But for Chicago's unpretentious blue-collar workers, the ones who drank beer in the South Side gin mills, Comiskey Park was a field of dreams.

Chicago began planning its new stadium in the late 1980s, when Chisox management threatened to move the team to Tampa if better accommodations were not forthcoming. A parking garage is now being built where the old ball yard once stood.

Comiskey Park, with its rusting girders and cracking concrete, probably needed replacement. Nonetheless, the Windy City has lost one of its most famous landmarks.

On September 30, 1990, the ballpark's last day of operation, the management thanked the Chisox fans for the many pleasant memories.

(Left) *Fans enjoy the action at Comiskey Park during a 1984 contest.*

President Harry S Truman tosses out the ceremonial first ball for the opening game of the 1951 season at Griffith Stadium, while Senators manager Bucky Harris, Yankee manager Casey Stengel, and other dignitaries look on.

One of Griffith Stadium's greatest moments came on April 17, 1953, when Yankee slugger Mickey Mantle belted out a mammoth home run that landed in the yard of a house across the street from the stadium. The arrow in this photo shows the orbit of the blast. Numbers 1 and 2 mark long home runs hit by Larry Doby and Babe Ruth, respectively.

GRIFFITH
STADIUM
Washington, D. C.

1911–1961

This photo shows the Washington Senators and the New York Giants in action at Griffith Stadium during the 1924 World Series, which Washington won four games to three.

U **NTIL 1961,** the land occupied by Griffith Stadium had been home to one major league baseball team or another since 1892. A year before that, in 1891, 125 oak trees had been cleared on the grounds to create Boundary Field, also known as National Park when a National League franchise, called the Senators, played there during the late 1890s. That club eventually folded, but the Washington Senators of the three-year-old American League occupied the park in 1904. On March 17, 1911, the wooden grandstands around the field were destroyed by fire, and the Senators began building the ballpark that later became known as Griffith Stadium.

The Senators' new field was ready for play two weeks after the fire, though the double-deck, 27,410-seat, concrete grandstand was not completed until midsummer. That delay set the pattern for additions and changes at Griffith over the course of the years. In fact, the park that some of today's fans still remember was built in piecemeal fashion during four decades. In 1920, the new team president, Clark Griffith expanded the two-tiered grandstand to the foul poles in right and left field. Bleacher seats were added at several intervals in the park's history, both to increase

Griffith Stadium's best player was Walter Johnson, winner of 416 games during his 21 seasons with Washington.

Washington Senators' owner Clark Griffith surveys the field before the opening game of the 1924 World Series.

the seating capacity and to bring the distant outfield fences closer to home plate.

Like so many of the old ballparks, Griffith Stadium had a playing surface marked by quirks and crannies. At one time, the path from home plate to first base ran downhill to assist slow-footed Senator batters as they ambled along the line. In center field, there was a small box to hold the American flag when it was not being flown, and that box—called "the Dog House"—was in the area of play. According to baseball lore, the door of the Dog House was once accidentally left open before a game, and, of course, a batted ball, hotly pursued by a Philadelphia Athletics center fielder, rolled in. The fielder got stuck in the box while the Senator hitter circled the bases for an inside-the-park homer.

The outfield fences at Griffith Stadium contained an assortment of heights and angles, which made earning a living difficult for Senators and visiting outfielders alike. The wooden fence in front of the bullpen in right center field was only four feet high, while the concrete wall in left field was 12 feet and the barrier in right loomed 30 feet above the field. The scoreboard in right center was even higher, and it was topped by an advertising sign that once featured a three-dimensional National Bohemian beer bottle whose cap extended 56 feet above the ground. In center field, the wall jutted sharply inward in deference to five houses and a huge tree that stood just outside the park. A ball hit off the center field angle might carom in any direction.

Because of its distance from home plate, however, that crooked wall did not often come into play. Griffith Stadium, like Forbes

Hall of Famer Leon "Goose" Goslin played for the Senators from 1921 until 1930. In the pennant-winning season of 1924, Goslin drove in a league-leading 129 runs.

Field in Pittsburgh, was a classic pitcher's park. Until the left field fence was brought closer to the plate in 1952, a batted ball had to travel more than 400 feet to reach it. The distance to the wall in left center field and center ranged from 391 feet to 457 feet, requiring a mighty poke from even the most powerful hitter. The fence in right and right center ranged from 320 feet to 378 feet, but the 30-foot-high wall there made homers difficult. Home runs in Griffith Stadium were so infrequent, in fact, that during the entire 1945 season, the Senators hit only one four-bagger there—an inside-the-park homer.

Not surprisingly, the best player in Washington Senator history was a pitcher—Walter "Big Train" Johnson, who pitched for the team from 1907 to 1927, winning 416 games, more than any major leaguer except Cy Young, and amassing lifetime statistics that will never be matched. In 12 seasons he won 20 or more games and twice he topped the 30-win mark. A dozen times he led American League moundsmen in strikeouts. Eleven times his year-end earned run average was below 2.00; in

Sam Rice, the Senators' outfielder, scores a first-inning run during game two of the 1924 World Series. A ticket from the Series is shown above.

Josh Gibson: Negro League Slugger

Griffith Stadium's most feared slugger was not a Washington Senator. It was Josh Gibson of the Negro League's Homestead Grays.

Gibson was the Negro League's Babe Ruth, a powerful right-handed-hitting catcher whose seasonal and lifetime home run marks are the stuff of legend. Born in Georgia, Gibson grew up in Pittsburgh, where his father had taken a job in a steel mill. Although Josh was still a teenager when he signed with the Homestead Grays in 1930, he quickly proved himself to be the most awesome slugger in the land, socking 60 or 70 homers per year and launching tape-measure blasts that are still discussed by fans of the old Negro League.

From 1937 through 1948, the Grays played a portion of their home games at Griffith Stadium. Twice Gibson cleared the wall behind the stadium's left field bleachers, a feat accomplished by only one other player before or since—Mickey Mantle. Clark Griffith, the Senators' owner, once quipped that during the early 1940s Gibson hit more homers into those distant left field seats than did the whole American League. Griffith may not have been exaggerating.

In 1943, after the wartime draft had decimated major league rosters, Griffith asked Gibson and his teammate Buck Leonard if they were interested in playing for the Senators. Gibson and Leonard responded affirmatively, but Griffith never pursued the matter. By 1947, when Jackie Robinson played his first major league game, it was too late for Gibson. He died on January 20 of that year, at age 35.

1913, when he won 36, it was a miniscule 1.09.

Unfortunately, Johnson pitched for bad teams. As the saying went, Washington was "first in war, first in peace, and last in the American League." During the Senators' first quarter-century of play, not a single championship pennant flew over Griffith Stadium, despite Johnson's efforts. In fact, the team rarely finished above fourth place. At age 36, after 17 years of service, Big Train had still not competed in World Series play.

In 1924, however, the Senators made a run for the American League flag. Johnson won 23 games that season and led the league in earned run average. Goose Goslin drove home a league-leading 129 runs, and Sam Rice topped the loop with 216 hits. Of course, with Griffith Stadium as their home park, the Senators hit only 22 homers—Babe Ruth alone hit 46 that year for the Yankees—but they beat the Bronx Bombers by two games to clinch the league championship. Finally, Big Train would compete in a Fall Classic. His opponents would be John McGraw's New York Giants.

Perhaps it was the pressure of a long-awaited dream finally coming true, but Johnson failed in his first two World Series starts. He lost the opener by a score of 4-3 in 12 innings and was battered 6-2 in game five. But, with the Series tied after six games he got another chance to rise to the occasion. In game seven, at Griffith Stadium, he watched from the bench for eight innings. In the ninth, with the score knotted in a 3-3 tie, manager Bucky Harris turned to him to stop the Giants. Big Train held the New Yorkers for four innings. Then, in the 12th frame, the Senators put two men aboard. Earl McNeely smashed a double-play grounder toward third base, but the ball struck a pebble and bounded over Fred Lindstrom's head into left field. The winning run raced home, and Johnson had his first World Series championship. The next season, the

Groundskeepers remove team insignias from the grounds after the conclusion of the last game at Griffith Stadium on September 21, 1961. The park hosted its first game in 1911.

Senators won another pennant, and Johnson pitched two victories in the Series, but this time his efforts were in a losing cause.

Though Griffith Stadium history is dominated by Johnson's pitching heroics, one of the park's greatest moments belongs to a slugger—Mickey Mantle. On April 17, 1953, the visiting Yankee blasted a mammoth home run that cleared the back wall of the left field bleachers and landed in the yard of a house across the street from the stadium. It measured 565 feet. Old-timers say that only Josh Gibson, who played at Griffith Stadium during the 1940s when the park hosted the Homestead Grays of the old Negro League, hit a ball as far.

The Senators used Griffith Stadium until 1960, when, after several losing seasons and dwindling attendance, they left for Minnesota. A new Washington Senators team appeared in the league in 1961, but it used the old park for only one season before moving to D. C. Stadium (later RFK Stadium) on the Anacostia River. In 1965, earth movers and wrecking balls reduced Griffith Stadium to rubble. Today, Howard University Hospital stands on the place where Walter Johnson performed his great pitching feats.

The Griffith Stadium site is now occupied by Howard University Hospital.

The formidable John McGraw, elected to the Hall of Fame in 1937, played major league ball for 16 years and managed the Giants from 1902 through 1932.

THE POLO GROUNDS

New York, New York

1911–1957, 1962–1963

This 1938 photo of a Giants-Phillies game offers a good view of the Polo Grounds' outfield. Note the close left field wall, over which Bobby Thomson arched his "home run heard 'round the world" in 1951, and the deep center field barrier that gave Willie Mays the running room he needed to make "the Catch" in 1954.

IT WAS USED for football, track and field, boxing, tennis, midget auto racing, and soccer, as well as thousands of baseball games, but a polo mallet never thwacked a ball at the Harlem baseball field known as the Polo Grounds. The long-time home of the Giants and the field used by the pre-Shea-Stadium Mets was named for an earlier ballpark on 6th Avenue and 110th Street. That park, which consisted of two fields separated by a canvas barrier, had been built on land owned by James Gordon Bennett, Jr., a New York businessman who used his property for polo matches. Hence, the name.

Those first Polo Grounds, which were used in the 1880s by the American Association's Metropolitans and the National League's Giants, saw some wondrous sights, including the first "World Series"—a three-out-of-five contest between the National League's Providence Grays and the Metropolitans in 1884—and the slugging of the Giants' dead-ball-era home run king, Roger Connor (136 homers between 1880 and 1897). But by 1888 both of the original Polo Grounds' diamonds had been abandoned, its teams playing elsewhere.

The Polo Grounds at Coogan's Bluff that many of

Giants owner Horace Stoneham (right) watches as Bernard Deutsch, president of the Board of Aldermen, throws out the ceremonial first ball on opening day at the Polo Grounds in 1934.

In what was one of the Polo Ground's most memorable moments, Bobby Thomson completes his circuit around the bases in the wake of his home run in the last inning of the last game of the 1951 National League playoffs. This program is from a Polo Grounds game that same year.

today's fans still remember opened in 1890 as Brotherhood Park and was used for a year by the Giants of the short-lived Players' League. After one season that circuit failed, and the National League Giants, who were playing at an adjacent park called Manhattan Field, moved in. Thereafter, the field became known as the New Polo Grounds. The great Christy Mathewson started his career there, and the park also witnessed the "Merkle Boner," when in the tight pennant race of 1908, Giant rookie Fred Merkle failed to touch second base as his teammate scored the apparent winning run in a crucial September game against the Cubs. The mistake cost the Giants the pennant.

In April 1911, a severe fire damaged that park, and the Giants' owner, John T. Brush, decided to rebuild on the same spot using the new, steel-and-concrete style of stadium construction that was then replacing the old tinderboxes of the day. The new park with its horseshoe-shaped, double-deck grandstand opened on June 28, 1911, though construction continued through mid-October, when the Giants lost to the Philadelphia Athletics in the World Series.

From the beginning, the new Polo Grounds' field had a shape that was much better suited to football than baseball, its form being dictated by the hollow in which it sat. Over the years, several changes were made in the field to accommodate fans and

players, but looking at it as it was in the late 1940s—the time when it would be recalled by most people alive now—the dimensions were as follows: 280 feet in left field, 455 feet at the right of the bullpen in left center, 505 feet in center (reduced to 483 in 1954), 449 feet at the bullpen in right center, and 258 feet at the pole in right.

The peculiar dimensions of the field came to have a decisive influence on play at the Polo Grounds. If, for example, a batter could hit a pop fly down either line, he might have an easy home run. Or consider the upper grandstand in left field, which protruded 23 feet over the field of play. If a ball were hit 250 feet into the air in left field, a fielder could stand in play and wait for the ball to descend, only to see it fall safely into the stands above his head. While left field was rosy for right-handed hitters, the fences were beyond reach for any but the mightiest of sluggers everywhere else. Center field was such a distance from home plate that for a while, before legendary manager John McGraw ordered them removed, there were flower beds out there. Luke Easter blasted a shot into the center field bleachers in 1948 in a Negro League game, a feat matched only three other times—by Joe Adcock, Lou Brock, and Henry Aaron. The latter two were facing hapless New York Mets pitchers, but that tarnishes the feat only slightly.

The two most famous incidents ever to occur within the Polo Grounds' walls were directly attributable to the park's ovoid shape. The first, which came to be known as "the shot heard round the world," occurred in 1951. Despite high hopes and the acquisition of Willie Mays, the Giants were 13 1/2 games behind the league-leading Dodgers on August 12, the day Brooklyn manager Charlie Dressen—who had clearly never read Greek literature or learned English grammar—announced, "The Giants is dead." But then the Dodgers slumped and the Giants soared. The season ended in a dead heat. A two-out-of-three series would be needed to decide which team would face the New York Yankees in the World Series. The Giants playing in Ebbets Field won the first contest by a score of 3-1 on a two-run homer by Bobby Thomson off Ralph Branca. The Dodgers stormed back and took the second game at the Polo Grounds 10-0.

This unusual shot taken from the center field bleachers shows Willie Mays making what is simply called "the Catch." Mays' remarkable ballhandling turned out to be the pivotal moment in the first game of the 1954 World Series, and ultimately in the Series itself.

But the third game saw a ninth-inning shot by Thomson off Branca fly over the left field wall to give the Giants a 5-4 victory. Is there a Dodger fan born before 1945 who does not get outraged just thinking of announcer Russ Hodges screaming "THE GIANTS WIN THE PENNANT! THE GIANTS WIN THE PENNANT! THE GIANTS WIN THE PENNANT!" as Thomson circled the bases? Even Giants manager Leo Durocher admitted, "In any other ballpark in the country, the left fielder would have come in a few steps to catch it."

The second most celebrated event to occur at the Polo Grounds, "the Catch," occurred in 1954, during game one of the last World Series played at the ballpark. It came in the top of the eighth inning, with the score tied at two and nobody out. Larry Doby was on second base, Al Rosen on first, and Cleveland's Vic Wertz, with already three hits that day, faced Giant reliever Don Liddle. Liddle threw his first and only pitch of the day, a shoulder-high fastball that Wertz sent screaming into deepest center field.

Willie Mays ran after the drive, head down, not even looking at the flight of the ball. At the last moment, he caught it over his left shoulder and, in the same motion, heaved it toward the infield, his cap flying, as he fell to the ground. Mays' throw held Rosen at first base, and Larry Doby advanced only to third. Neither man scored, and Dusty Rhodes' 10th-inning single gave the Giants the game. Demoralized, the Indians dropped the next three contests.

That was the last year of Giants glory. In 1955, the team finished in third place, then fell to sixth in 1956 and 1957. Fans stopped coming to the Polo Grounds, and those who did venture forth feared for their safety, as box seat ticketholders were get-

The Amazin' Mets at the Polo Grounds

The New York Giants were so good for so long that they had players who did not even need second names: Christy, Leo, Willie. If you know baseball, you know who these fellows were and how great were their contributions to the game.

The Mets also played in the Giants' old home, the Polo Grounds, during the team's first two frustrating years of existence. The names of few of those early Mets endure—except for those of old stars whose reputations had already been made. Most were has-beens, some were never-were's, and many were wouldn't-be's. But the memory of their ineptitude lingers, like the smell of neat's-foot oil as it is rubbed lovingly into a new glove. Roger Angell, one of this (or any) generation's greatest and most erudite baseball writers, tells the following story in his book Five Seasons. It typifies the quality of play displayed by the Mets during their two summers in the Polo Grounds.

Richie Ashburn, a once-talented center fielder playing his last season as a Met, was constantly being knocked to the ground as he waited for fly balls in short center field. He would camp under the ball and shout the traditional "I got it! I got it!" only to be bulldozed by Elio Chacon, the team's Venezuelan shortstop. Ashburn tried to explain that when he yelled "I got it!" it meant that Chacon should back off, but it did no good; the enthusiastic and likable Chacon continued to knock the veteran off of his feet in a vain attempt to catch the

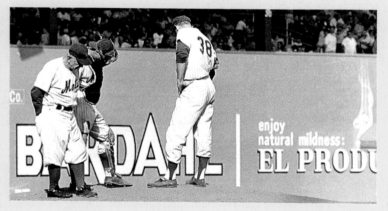

During the Mets' Polo Grounds years, this was a typical scene: Casey Stengel—probably wondering "Can't anybody here play this game?"—removing pitcher Roger Craig from the contest.

ball, which would inevitably fall to the ground. Finally, Ashburn went to a bilingual colleague for advice and was told, next time, to shout Yo la tengo! Yo la tengo!, which roughly means "I got it! I got it!" in Spanish.

In the second or third inning of the next game, a batter hit a fly to short center. Ashburn got smartly under it, remembering to yell, Yo la tengo! Yo la tengo! Chacon appropriately backed off. Ashburn waited to make the easy catch and was leveled by Frank Thomas, the Mets' left fielder who spoke not a word of Spanish.

ting mugged right in the park. After 1957, the Giants departed for San Francisco, and the great ballpark saw no more baseball until the expansion Mets played there in 1962 and 1963. The newcomers were fun to watch, but managed to win only 91 games while losing 231 during those two seasons. In 1964, the park was demolished. Four 30-story buildings now stand on the old site. They are called the Polo Grounds Housing Project.

The venerable ballpark was dismantled in 1964, after the Mets moved to Shea Stadium. In its place, high-rise apartments, similar to those in the background, were erected.

Paul Derringer had great success pitching in this tiny, bandbox ballpark; he won 20 games four times during his 10 seasons with the Reds.

Hall of Fame catcher Ernie Lombardi batted .300 seven times during his ten Cincinnati summers, including a league-leading .342 in 1938.

CROSLEY FIELD
Cincinnati, Ohio

1912–1970

Three ballparks were erected on the same piece of land in downtown Cincinnati between 1884 and 1902. Then what became known as Crosley Field opened in 1912 and served as home for the Cincinnati Reds for 58 years.

7HE PIECE OF LAND in downtown Cincinnati where Findlay and Western Avenues meet was the site of four ballparks, hosting major league baseball from 1884 through 1970. The first, built by Aaron Stein for his American Association Reds and named the Cincinnati Base Ball Grounds (later called Western Avenue Grounds or League Park), was so hastily erected that a grandstand collapsed on opening day, killing one fan and injuring many others. The park was reconstructed for the National League's Reds in 1894, but fires in 1900 and 1901 so damaged the facility that it had to be torn down. The next season, a totally rebuilt, vastly improved ballpark opened and was grandiloquently named the Palace of the Fans. It had a Roman-like interior, with handsome columns and a pointed pediment over the roof behind home plate. In 1911, it too burned, necessitating the creation of a fourth ballpark on the same grounds, Redland Field (later changed to Crosley Field by the automobile builder, Powell Crosley, after he purchased the Reds in 1934).

The new stadium opened with full pomp and circumstance on May 18, 1912. Two prominent American Leaguers were in attendance, Ban Johnson, the league's

Powell Crosley, the automobile manufacturer who purchased the Reds in 1934, chats with manager Bill McKechnie before the third game of the 1939 World Series at Crosley Field.

founder and president, and Charles Comiskey, the owner of the Chicago White Sox. Johnson had started his career as a Cincinnati sportswriter, and the Old Roman had managed the Reds in the 1890s. This field, in modified form, would serve as the home park of the Reds for the next 58 years.

Built into the heart of an urban complex of streets, Crosley Field had the shape of the surrounding neighborhood. Originally, the park played large—360 feet from home plate to the foul lines and 420 feet in dead center field. But in 1925, new seats were installed, reducing the dimensions of the field. Crosley added more seats in 1935 and 1939, giving his park its final form. With these additions, the seating capacity was fixed at about 29,600, and the dimensions of the playing area were set at 328 feet to left field, 382 feet to the enormous scoreboard in left center, and 387 in center. Only the home run distance in right field and right center fluctuated with the addition and removal of a temporary fence. Overall, the park was small. Consequently hitters loved the place and pitchers hated it. Outfielders sided with the pitchers, for, instead of a warning track in front of the outfield walls, Crosley Field featured a steep grassy incline, which made an adventure of every fly ball hit near the wall.

On May 24, 1935, Crosley Field was the site of the first night game in major league history; the Reds lost to the Philadelphia Phillies by a score of 2–1.

Over the years, Crosley Field became known as the home of baseball firsts. Actually, it merely upheld an honorable Cincinnati tradition. The city was the home of the first professional baseball team, the 1869 Cincinnati Red Stockings, who barnstormed around the country taking on the local champions and winning 92 straight games. The Red Stockings were charter members of the National League in 1876 (but they were expelled after the 1880 season for allowing Sunday games and selling beer). And a Cincinnati team finished first in the American Association's inaugural year, 1882.

Crosley Field added to the tradition of Cincinnati firsts by being the first major league park to be leased to a Negro League team when the Cuban Stars used the field during the 1920s. In 1929, the Cincinnati Reds became the first team to air games on a regular basis over the radio. Skeptics were convinced that this was the beginning of the end of live attendance.

Crosley Field was also the site of the first big league baseball game played at night. With Cincinnati still suffering from the effects of the Great Depression, the Reds' General Manager, Larry MacPhail, one of baseball's great innovators, convinced other league owners that unless they allowed night baseball in his city, the team would fold because of low attendance. Rather than see that, the other owners agreed to allow the innovation, and on May 24, 1935, the first major league night game was played at Crosley. President Franklin Roosevelt threw a switch in the White House to turn on

Hard-hitting Frank Robinson led the Reds to the pennant in 1961 and also took home the National League's Most Valuable Player Award.

the lights, and baseball after dark—a blessing and a curse to fan and player alike—had begun.

The penultimate night game of that 1935 season saw another first: the first woman in a major league batter's box. Kitty Burke, a publicity-hungry entertainer, rushed onto the field before a standing-room crowd, took a bat from Babe Herman, and urged Paul Dean to pitch to her. Dean, who was nicknamed "Daffy" for a reason, obliged her, and she managed to ground out, pitcher to first base, while the appreciative crowd roared.

Crosley was also probably the first baseball field onto which players rowed. That noteworthy event took place in January 1937 when Mill Creek overflowed its banks sufficiently to cover the stadium's outfield wall. Two Reds' pitchers, Lee Grissom and Gene Schott, pulling off a publicity stunt, were photographed in uniform rowing a small boat over the wall onto the field.

Four World Series were played at Crosley Field, and, again, one of them was a first. In 1919, the Reds took the National League pennant and, to almost everyone's surprise, defeated the powerful White Sox five games to three. Later, an investigation revealed that eight Chicago players had conspired to throw the Series. This was the first and only time that major league players have been caught tampering with the

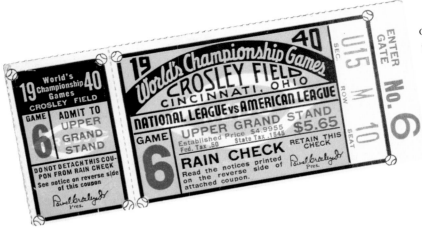

The holder of this 1940 World Series ticket saw Buckey Walters shut out the Tigers on four hits.

outcome of the Fall Classic. (See chapter on old Comiskey Park in this volume.)

The Reds played in the Series again in 1939, but this time they were swept by the Yankees. In the final game, catcher Ernie Lombardi was dazed after a collision with hulking outfielder Charlie "King Kong" Keller. While Lombardi was semiconscious, Joe DiMaggio raced home with the final run in a three-run 10th inning. The demoralized Reds could not recover, and the Yanks became World Champs. But Crosley fans had more to cheer about the next October as the Reds defeated the Tigers in seven games.

In 1961, Frank Robinson led the Reds to another pennant, but this time Cincinnati's timing was wrong. The Reds had to play the 1961 Yankees of Roger Maris and Mickey Mantle. They managed to last five games before capitulating—in humiliating fashion. After splitting the first two games in the Bronx, the Reds lost all three contests in front of their hometown fans. Never again would the Reds take a pennant at Crosley.

The Big Red Machine of the 1970s played in their new digs, Riverfront Stadium. Inadequate seating capacity, a decaying neighborhood, and poor parking and public transportation had doomed the old site. In Crosley's last game, on June 24, 1970, the Reds defeated the Giants by a score of 5-4. They played before a crowd of more than 28,000 fans who had come to say goodbye to the park of firsts.

Bucky Walters, who won 20 games for the Reds three times, pitched two complete-game victories in the 1940 World Series.

The 1940 World Series

Reds' second baseman Eddie Joost tags out Detroit's Hank Greenberg during game seven of the 1940 World Series at Crosley Field. The Reds won the game behind Paul Derringer by a score of 2–1.

The fan who held this 1961 World Series ticket saw the Yankees' Whitey Ford and Jim Coates combine for a five-hit shut out.

The Cincinnati Reds won two World Series during their Crosley Field seasons. The first, in 1919, was tainted: eight members of the opposing Chicago White Sox allegedly conspired to lose the championship. The Reds' 1940 victory over the Tigers, however, was legitimate.

The Series opened at Crosley Field, with Detroit's Bobo Newsom taming the Reds by a score of 7-2. Cincinnati's starter, 20-game-winner Paul Derringer, did not last the second inning. But the next day the Reds evened the Series behind their 22-game winner, Bucky Walters. Then the Series moved to Detroit, where the Tigers won two out of three games. One of them marked a victory for Derringer, who avenged his defeat in game one.

Down 3-2 in the Series, the Reds needed to win twice in Crosley Field to avoid their second straight World Series disappoint-ment. In game six, Walters, the game-two winner, was up to the task, going the distance and shut-ting out the Tigers on only five hits. The Series was then even with a seventh game in the offing.

In game seven, it was Der-ringer again for the Reds and New-som for Detroit. Bobo had already racked up two Series victories, and another would make him this Oc-tober's hero. But both pitchers were at their best. Going into the seventh inning, Detroit was ahead by a score of 1-0. In the seventh frame, however, the Reds rallied for two runs to take a lead they would not surrender. Derringer and Newsom went the distance, but the Reds' righthander was just a bit better. Derringer and Walters, the National League's two best pitchers in 1940, had brought a second World Championship to Crosley Field, and this one was not tainted.

On April 19, 1972, the demolition of Crosley Field began. Ironically, this photo shows the wreckers's ball—painted to resemble a baseball—pounding an emblem that commemorated the Reds' 100th anniversary.

Fenway's left field wall—"the Green Monster"—is 37 feet high and reportedly 315 feet from home plate.

Carl Yastrzemski grabs one over his head in front of Fenway's hand-operated scoreboard in left field during the fifth inning of the first game of the 1967 World Series.

FENWAY PARK
Boston, Massachusetts

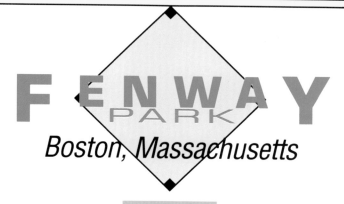

1912–

This recent shot of Fenway Park shows that the old ballpark is still in magnificent condition.

FENWAY PARK, one of the few examples of a pre-World War I, steel-and-concrete ballpark still in use—Wrigley Field and Tiger Stadium are the others—is a cherished New England institution. It was built for the opening of the 1912 season. Prior to that, the Boston Red Sox had been playing in the Huntington Avenue Grounds, a wooden firetrap that had become an embarrassment to the team and the town. To rectify the situation, club owner John I. Taylor bought land for his new park from his own family, began construction on the stadium, and then sold the team before the work was completed. He grew richer by the transaction and so did Boston.

The Sox won the first game in their new park against the New York Highlanders (known since 1913 as the Yankees) by a score of 7-6 in 11 innings. They went on to win the American League pennant that year as well, their first since 1904. So good were the 1912 Sox that the team has still not duplicated its record—105 wins and only 47 losses. Smokey Joe Wood won 34 games, and Tris Speaker hit .383.

Many old-timers call the 1912 World Series the most exciting in history. Those who remember the October

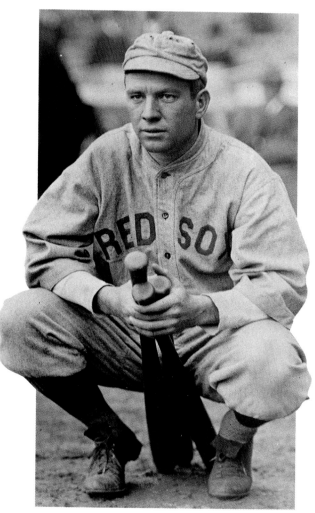

Tris Speaker, who played for the Red Sox from 1907 until 1915, twice led the American League in doubles. His heroics in the final game of the 1912 World Series saved the championship for the Sox.

This photo captures a beloved baseball tradition—Old-Timer's Day—with Hall of Famer Bobby Doerr signing autographs for the Fenway fans before the former greats' game in 1987.

Ted Williams, "the Splendid Splinter," was the Red Sox' best hitter and the last major leaguer to bat .400 in a season—.406 in 1941.

Classics of 1975 and 1986—which also featured the Red Sox—might disagree, but the 1912 epic, especially the final game, was remarkable. The Sox beat John McGraw's New York Giants at the Polo Grounds in the first game by a single run. The second game, at Fenway, resulted in a 6-6 tie after 11 innings when nightfall brought an end to play. Game three, still at Fenway, was won by New York by a score of 2-1 when outfielder Josh Devore made a running catch in the bottom of the ninth inning with two outs and two men on base to preserve the victory. The teams split the next four games, setting the stage for the climactic eighth and final game at Fenway.

In the deciding contest, Mc-Graw pitched his ace, Christy Mathewson. The Giants scored in the third inning; the Sox matched them with a run in the seventh. That's where things stood after nine, but New York broke the tie with a run in the top of the 10th. Then Boston came to bat. First up was pinch hitter Clyde Engle, who popped a lazy fly ball to center fielder Fred Snodgrass . . . who dropped it. Engle was safe at first. Then Harry Hooper allowed Snodgrass to almost redeem himself with a sinking line drive but the center fielder caught the ball in spectacular fashion, giving the Sox their first out. The next batter walked. With two men on base, the indomitable Speaker came to bat, but he popped a foul along the first base line, an easy out for either catcher Chief Meyers or first baseman Fred Merkle, except that the ball fell between them, each expecting the other to catch it. Not wasting his godsend, Speaker ripped the next pitch into right field, bringing in Engle, Snodgrass' gift, to tie the score. With runners on second and third, McGraw ordered Mathewson to walk the next batter, Heinie Wagner, but this strategy was nullified when Larry Gardner brought in the game winner with a sacrifice fly, giving the Sox the victory by a score of 3-2. It was a wonderful way to celebrate the inaugural year of Fenway.

The dimensions of Fenway Park correspond exactly to the irregular street pattern bordering its outer walls. The right field foul pole is only 302 feet from home plate, and the wall there is less than six feet high. A simple slice in the right direction and a batter can add a home run to his record. But then the boundaries slope steeply outward from the plate, totaling 380 feet at the bullpens in front of the right field bleachers. Originally deep right field had been 405 feet, but in 1940 the pens were added, cutting 25 feet from the distance Ted Williams had to reach for one of his homers. For the next 20 years, the pens were appropriately called "Williamsburg." Adjacent to the bullpens and bleachers, a triangle of turf extends 420 feet from the plate in straightaway center field. (In the early 1930s, this distance was 593 feet.) A modern—some would say an inappropriately modern—scoreboard looms over and behind the right field bleacher seats. Around the whole park, the grandstands hug the field closely. All in all, the ballpark provides a cozy, close-to-the-game environment.

Oh yes, and in left field, there is the enormous green Wall. The Wall dominates the park, the most idiosyncratic element in a completely idiosyncratic field. At its base is a scoreboard, one of the last of the hand-operated scoreboards in the majors. Its only concession to modernity is its use of green and red lights to signal balls, strikes, and outs. On the right side of the scoreboard are mysterious dots and dashes that spell out in Morse Code TAY and JRY, the initials of Tom and Jean Yawkey, who bought the team and refurbished the park in 1933. A ladder is built into the wall so that groundskeepers can retrieve balls hit over the 37-foot "Green Monster" into the 23-foot screen that Yawkey put up to protect windows on the other side of Lansdowne Street. Green paint was first applied in 1934, replacing a plethora of advertising billboards that used to plaster the surface. Officially the wall is 315 feet from home plate, but an independent researcher measured it as 309 feet, 5 inches. To resolve the controversy, the Boston Globe used aerial photography and the principles of trigonometry to compute a distance of only 304.8 feet. No wonder southpaws feel the Wall loom over their shoulders as they nervously stare at Boston's right-handed batters.

The Wall affects play in a variety of ways. Shots 20 feet high and rising as they hit the Wall bounce back, and a good left fielder (say, Ted Williams or Carl Yastrzemski) can keep the batter to a single, rather than the homer he would have had in a "normal" park. But what the Wall taketh away, the Wall also giveth. Bucky Dent, the light-hitting shortstop of the 1978 Yankees, poked a game-winning, pop-fly home run into the screen in the one-game playoff staged to settle the division championship that year. Boston fans would prefer to remember the sixth game of the 1975 World Series.

(Top) *This 1912 World Series "biography" and scorebook once sold for a dime.*

(Above) *Red Sox owners Tom and Jean Yawkey enjoy the action on opening day in 1934.*

The Greatest World Series Game

Many call the sixth game of the 1975 World Series at Fenway Park the greatest game in World Series history. It is somewhat ironic then that so many of the game's key plays were directly influenced by the configurations of the ballpark itself.

Game six began with the Red Sox trailing the Cincinnati Reds three games to two in the Series. Needing a win to force a seventh game the next evening, Boston struck first. Fred Lynn, the American League's Rookie of the Year and Most Valuable Player, blasted a three-run homer off of Gary Nolan in the very first inning. The Reds tied the game in the fifth frame when Ken Griffey tripled over Lynn's head in Fenway's deepest center field, as the Bosox wunderkind went crashing into the then-unpadded wall in a vain attempt to snag the ball. The Reds took the lead in the seventh inning, on George Foster's smash off of the same center field fence, and added another run in the eighth when Cesar Geronimo blooped a home run around Fenway's short right field foul pole. Boston's pitcher, Luis Tiant, hoary as Lynn was youthful, was removed from the game as a sure loser, but Bernie Carbo's eighth-inning pinch hit homer into the center field bleachers tied the score 6-6 and took "El Tiante" off the hook.

In the ninth inning, the Sox

Carlton Fisk, who has just popped one toward the left field foul pole in the 12th inning of the sixth game of the 1975 World Series, is urging the ball to stay fair, while Cincinnati pitcher Pat Darcy and catcher Johnny Bench look on glumly.

loaded the bases with no outs, but they could not score. In the 11th inning, with Griffey on first base and one out, the Reds' Joe Morgan hit a long drive to Fenway's deep right field. Scrambling backward, Dwight Evans grabbed the ball out of thin air, bounced off the outfield wall, and then whirled and threw to first baseman Carl Yastrzemski. Yaz wheeled around and pegged the ball to shortstop Rick Burleson, who was covering first, to complete the inning-ending double play. At some point during all this action, Pete Rose turned to Bosox backstop Carlton Fisk and said, "This is some kind of game, isn't it?"

In the 12th frame, Pat Darcy, the Reds' eighth pitcher, faced Fisk. At exactly 12:34 a.m. Eastern Time, the Boston catcher lofted a high fly to the left field corner, the shortest part of the park. Whether it would stay fair or hook foul, no one could say. Fisk, skipping sideways, waved the ball fair until he saw it hit the mesh attached to the foul pole, and then danced around the bases while organist John Kiley played the opening chords of "The Hallelujah Chorus." That foul pole is supposedly 315 feet from home plate but is actually shorter. Still, a homer is a homer; and yes, Mr. Rose, that was some kind of game!

Called by some the most exciting World Series game in history, this seesaw struggle was won in the 12th inning when Carlton Fisk blooped one just fair over the Wall. The image of this enormous man, jogging sideways, pushing the ball fair with body English, is one of the indelible

The holder of this 1975 World Series ticket saw Luis Tiant tame the powerful Cincinnati Reds by a score of 6-0.

memories of anyone who stayed up well past midnight on the East Coast to see it.

In 1947, the temptingly close left field of Fenway and the seductively close right field of Yankee Stadium once put Yawkey and Yankee-owner Dan Topping, slightly in their cups, to thinking: what if we traded lefty Ted Williams for righty Joe DiMaggio? The agreement was reached and the next morning, when both were sober again, mutually abrogated. Often enough players are brought to teams because of the configurations of the ballpark. In this case, however, common sense (and, presumably, a fear of lynching)prevented the two premier hitters of their day from playing home games in the parks most suited to their abilities.

During the 1960s, many franchises abandoned their cozy, inner-city ballparks in favor of large suburban stadiums. But the Red Sox decided to remain in their 34,000-seat brick home wedged between Lansdowne and Van Ness streets. Boston fans pray that their Sox will stay in Fenway forever.

This shot, taken from Van Ness Street, shows Fenway Park's classic brick facade.

Fenway's bleachers fans of today may not be as well-dressed as the ones in this 1946 photo, but the hot dogs are still a big seller at the old park.

A snarling Tiger insignia greets those who enter the Tiger Stadium offices.

Team owner Frank Navin watches as Ty Cobb signs his 1919 contract with the Tigers. Cobb would take his 12th batting crown that year with a .382 average.

TIGER STADIUM
Detroit, Michigan

1912–

7IGER STADIUM is like the house that Jack built. Its location has always remained the same, but the structure keeps getting bigger (and the name keeps changing). It started out in 1901 as Bennett Park, a typical wooden structure of the day, named after Charley Bennett, a catcher for the team when it played in the National League as the Wolverines (Bennett had lost both of his legs in a train accident in 1894). The place held only 8,500 spectators, and only inches below the loam and grass were the cobblestones of the park's previous incarnation as a hay market. As every gardener knows, stones usually work their way to the surface, so sliding into bases and fielding grounders were not always pleasant experiences in Bennett Park.

In 1907, the park was enlarged by the removal of a mill that had acted as the left field wall. In addition, the fences were pushed back so that the outfield could accommodate more standees. For the 1908 season, team owner Frank Navin boosted the seating capacity to 10,000 (although more than 14,000 fans were shoehorned in for opening day). Two years later, new grandstands were added, increasing the park's capacity by another 3,000.

Orange and blue plastic seats were installed in 1980, giving the old ballpark a bright, modern look.

Hall of Famer Al Kaline, a Tiger Stadium favorite, played for Detroit from 1953 through 1974 and retired with 399 lifetime homers.

From an engineering standpoint, the kind of jury-rigging that Bennett Park experienced could go only so far, so Navin decided to get rid of the dead wood and replace
it with a concrete-and-steel arena. In addition to removing the timber, he also reori-
ented the field by shifting home plate from what is now right field to its present location. At the same time, the park's name was changed to—what else?—Navin Field.
The project was completed for the 1912 season.

The new field seated 23,000 and cost a half-million 1912 dollars. (In 1977, the stadium's new press box alone cost $600,000, and the present scoreboard, erected in
1980, was priced at $2 million.) For the 1923
season, a second deck, horseshoeing around
home plate from first base to third, was installed, increasing the seating capacity to
30,000, though 40,884 eager fans jammed the
park early that season to see the Tigers beat
the Yankees—always worth the price of admission to Detroiters.

The last major changes in the old ballpark—along with Boston's Fenway, the oldest
park in continuous use in the major leagues—
were made in 1936 and 1938, when the team's
new president, Walter Briggs, added decks in
right and center fields and a bleacher section
in center. The facility, now fully enclosed, was
then duly called Briggs Stadium, until a new
owner, John Fetzer, dubbed it Tiger Stadium
on January 1, 1961. Finally, the old, splinter-
ridden, wooden seats were replaced by blue
and orange plastic models, and the park's pre-
sent-day appearance was fixed. Today, 53,000
Tiger boosters can jockey through the narrow
aisles, tunnels, and bridges to their seats, and
the lucky patrons do not even have to sit behind the multitudinous steel girders that
support the upper deck.

During all of these changes, the park's playing dimensions have fluctuated
wildly. Ty Cobb, Hank Greenberg, and Chet Lemon stood at the same home plate, but
the fences they aimed for were considerably different. Currently the left field fence is
340 feet from home, left center is 365 feet, straightaway center is 440 feet, right center
is 375 feet, and right is 325. Adjacent to the 440-foot mark in center field is a 125-foot-
high flagpole. Until recently, balls might hit the pole anywhere, then bounce back into
fair territory, and still be considered in play. Now a line is painted on the pole, and
balls that land above the demarcation are considered home runs.

In a park as venerable as Tiger Stadium, many great ballplayers have managed to
perform many great and unusual deeds. In 1934, "Ducky" Medwick of the visiting Cardinals was forced to leave the seventh game of the World Series after irate Tiger fans
pelted him with fruits and vegetables in the sixth inning. The next year, in the sixth
and final game of the Series, the Cubs' Stan Hack belted a triple with no outs in the
ninth inning, only to be stranded at third; in the bottom half of the inning, the Tigers
broke the 3-3 tie and took their first World Championship in five tries. Highlights of
more recent summers include Dennis McLain's 31 wins in 1968, the first 30-win year
in the major leagues since Dizzy Dean's in 1934, and Mark "the Bird" Fidrych's rookie
season, 1976, in which he won 19 games and the league ERA title—while talking ani-
matedly to the baseball.

But the greatest—and most loathed—Tiger was Ty Cobb, who played for the team
from 1905 to 1926. Until Pete Rose passed him in 1985, Cobb had the most lifetime
hits in the majors. Lou Brock had stolen another of Cobb's records in 1977, but Cobb's

Hammerin' Hank Greenberg

Of the many home run hitters who have played at Tiger Stadium, the one who comes to mind first is Hank Greenberg. Greenberg starred with Detroit from 1933 to 1946, with four years off during World War II, during which he saw combat in the Pacific theater.

A native New Yorker, Greenberg joined the Tigers in 1930, at age 19. After a single time at bat, he returned to the minor leagues, but he was back in Detroit for the 1933 campaign. He batted .301 that season with 12 home runs and 87 RBIs. A year later, he was one of the league's most feared sluggers with a .339 batting average, 63 doubles, 26 homers, and 139 RBIs.

In 1938, Greenberg just missed tying Ruth's home run record by belting out 58 round-trippers. Four times he led the American League in homers, twice in doubles, and four times in RBIs. His 183 RBIs in 1937, one shy of Lou Gehrig's American League record, is the third highest single-season total in baseball history. During the late 1930s and the 1940s, Tiger fans argued that Greenberg was the equal of Joe DiMaggio.

Playing during an era when it was acceptable for players to yell "Jewboy" or "Sheeny" from an opposing dugout, Greenberg—as intelligent and affable as Ty Cobb was mean and vicious—exhibited a grace and dignity on the field that made him one of the game's most popular players. He was elected to the Baseball Hall of Fame in 1956.

.367 lifetime batting average is still tops. He won a dozen batting titles, twice hitting more than .400. Although he was celebrated for his abilities, he was also notorious for his foul temper and cutthroat style of play. He sharpened his spikes to intimidate his opponents as he slid into base and had the ground before home plate soaked to slow his bunts and make fielders lose footing.

But it's not Cobb's bunts that people think of when Tiger Stadium is mentioned; it's the long home runs that have been blasted there. Perhaps the overhanging right field deck—which cuts by 10 feet the already short 325-foot distance from home—accounts for the many homers the stadium has seen, but there is more to it than that. Something else has to explain Babe Ruth's 1926 blast that landed two

(Previous page) *Willie Horton has just singled in the winning run on September 14, 1968, to give Denny McLain his 30th win of the season. McLain is being hugged by Al Kaline.*

Kirk Gibson celebrates his first-inning homer against the San Diego Padres in the fifth and final game of the 1984 World Series at Tiger Stadium.

(Right) Reggie Jackson's homer in the 1971 All-Star Game at Tiger Stadium caromed off a light tower like the one pictured here. A ticket from the game is seen below.

(Below right) This 1971 scorebook was available from Tiger Stadium vendors for just 35 cents.

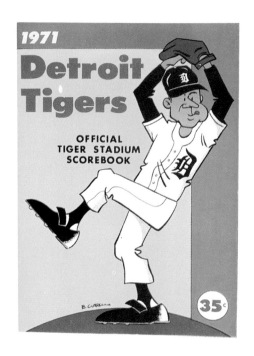

blocks away from deepest center field, some 800 feet from home plate; or Hank Greenberg's run at Ruth's single-season home run record in 1938; or Mickey Mantle's 1960 homer that was measured at 643 feet; or Reggie Jackson's mammoth shot off the light tower in the 1971 All-Star Game; or the fact that the 1987 Tigers hit more homers than any team in history except the 1961 Yankees of Mantle and Maris fame. Some-

Back from his four-year stint in the service, Hank Greenberg awaits a pitch from the Athletics' Bobo Newsom. Note the park's deep center field fence.

thing about Tiger Stadium, perhaps its colorful hitting background, brings out the best in sluggers. Just ask Cecil Fielder, the Tigers' first baseman, who in 1990 became the first player to hit 50 homers in a season since George Foster turned the trick in 1977.

The Tigers' last appearance in a World Series came in 1984, when the team rode a 35-5 start to the World Championship and when drunken louts celebrated the final Series win by going on a rampage, burning and destroying some of the neighborhood surrounding Tiger Stadium. Despite this unfortunate incident, the old park has a long and enviable record, one which Detroit's baseball fans appreciate. In 1974, John Fetzer turned down the chance to move his team to the suburban Silverdome. "This franchise," he said, "belongs to the inner city of Detroit; I'm just the caretaker." In 1986, when Mayor Coleman Young suggested demolishing Tiger Stadium in favor of a new dome, two-thirds of those asked by the Detroit Free Press opposed the move. An astute poll reader and shrewd politician, Young withdrew his suggestion, and the old park still stands. Whether it will continue to exist, however, remains in doubt. Recent talk suggests that with its lack of parking (and the awful things that happen to cars that do manage to find spots) as well as its deteriorating neighborhood, Tiger Stadium, home of much baseball glory, might soon be a thing of the past. It would be a pity.

Fans line up for a 1930 game at Ebbets Field.

EBBETS FIELD
Brooklyn, New York

Opening day activities for the brand-new Ebbets Field included this flag-raising ceremony.

7 **ECHNICALLY,** Brooklyn residents live in New York City. Until 1898, however, the borough was an independent city, and even today some Brooklynites still think of a trip to Manhattan as "going into the City." This spirit of independence explains in part why Dodger fans have never been able to forgive Walter O'Malley for pulling his team out of town in 1957. Could Brooklynites transfer their loyalty to the hated New York Yankees? Not a chance. Have the Mets succeeded in winning them over? Yes, to a degree, but it is not easy for Brooklyn's baseball fans to root for even a Queens-based team if it is called "New York."

Brooklyn's capital was Ebbets Field, the Valhalla destroyed in O'Malley's Götterdämmerung. Brooklynites found this ballpark particularly beautiful—a double-deck, enclosed grandstand set in an old but bustling neighborhood—but, in fact, it was like all parks. The grass was green, the earth was brown, and the walls were decorated with advertisements. The most famous of these were the ones for Schaefer beer—it also contained the indicator for hits and errors: the H lit up for one, and an E for the other—and for Abe Stark's suits. Stark was a Brooklyn

Charlie Ebbets, on the right, chats with Baseball Commissioner Kenesaw Mountain Landis.

haberdasher and Borough President whose billboard—"Hit this sign and get a free suit"—adorned the base of the right center field wall. The offer was a great gimmick, but Abe was on pretty safe ground. The angle that a ball had to traverse in order to hit the sign on a fly (an unspoken requirement) made it an easy catch for either center fielder Duke Snider or right fielder Carl Furillo.

The Dodgers' eventual departure for Los Angeles was foreshadowed in 1902, when the ballclub almost left Brooklyn for Baltimore. But Charley Ebbets, who had worked his way up in the Dodger organization from gofer to executive, bought the team and kept it home. The Dodgers—the sobriquet comes from having to dodge trolley cars near the ballpark—played in Washington Park, but it was an inadequate home and a wooden firetrap. Ebbets, determined to build a new park for his team and borough, searched Brooklyn until he found a piece of land in the Flatbush section that was used as a garbage dump—it was known as "Pigtown" because local swine had a tendency to dine there. But the plot was divided into parcels owned by 40 different people, and it took Ebbets more than three years to contact them all. He worked quietly, approaching each owner individually because he feared that if his reason for wanting the land became known, the prices for the outstanding parcels would go up.

Construction began in March 1912. The first league game was played on April 9, 1913, and the last, on September 24, 1957. The Dodgers lost the first one to the Phillies but ended their stay with a victory against lowly Pittsburgh. By that time, however, word of the defection was out, and apathy or anger kept the fans away; only 6,702 showed up.

Memory and romance have set the dimensions of the park as they were in the years of the Dodgers' greatest glories—the late 1940s through the mid-1950s—when the confines were to batters cozy and to pitchers a nightmare. As originally configured, the left field wall had been 419 feet from home, center field was 450 feet away (466 feet in 1930), and right center's deepest corner was 500 feet from the batter. Only the wall at the right field foul pole had always been short—301 feet originally. Over the years, the desire to increase seating capacity and other pressures conspired to bring the fences in. Left field was reduced to 343 feet

The man who broke baseball's color barrier, Jackie Robinson, is seen here with the man who brought him to the majors, Branch Rickey. Robinson is signing his 1949 contract, his third with the Brooklyn Dodgers.

This ticket is for the last Brooklyn Dodger baseball game played at Ebbets Field. Compare its price with that in the photo on page 66, taken 27 years earlier.

center field was cut down to 399 and that mammoth right center field meadow became a much more manageable 403 feet. Even shallow right field was reduced to 297.

Right field was a very exciting place for players as well as spectators. Directly behind it was Bedford Avenue, protected from the hazards of play by a 38-foot fence. The lower 19 feet of this structure were concave. They sloped away from the plate for the first 10 feet then went straight upward for the top nine. Atop this anomaly was a 19-foot screen. Unlike the comparable adornment above Fenway Park's left field wall, Ebbets Field's screen was in play. Balls that stuck in it were considered ground-rule doubles.

An early photo of Ebbets Field, which opened in 1913, shows fans arriving for a game. Note the Roman arches on the brick facade.

The Boys of Summer

There was magic at Ebbets Field during the 1950s. Campanella, Reese, Furillo, Hodges, Snider, and Robinson were helping the Dodgers win pennants, of course, but there was also a cast of hundreds in various supporting roles who fleshed out the park's special aura.

Tex Richards, the public address announcer, for example, was the master of malapropisms. "A little boy has been found lost," he once said. Another time he appealed to fans who were draping their shirts over an outfield wall: "Will the fans along the railing in left field please remove their clothes."

Ebbets Field was a bandbox ballpark complete with its own band, called "the Dodger Symphoney"— a host of fans who brought drums, cymbals, and trumpets to the park to torment opposition players and umpires. The world's greatest fan, Hilda Chester, resided in the bleachers with a cowbell in each hand. She would clang those bells in lieu of clapping when things went well or when she was trying to encourage a rally.

Despite the special aura that surrounded them, the Dodgers of the 1950s were a Greek tragedy waiting to unfold. Each year they seemed like noble Hector facing the terrible Achilles of the Bronx in single and unequal combat. Only once, in 1955, did the "good guys" beat the Yankees and win the World Series.

To make matters worse, for these boys of summer, autumn came very early. Personal tragedy found them with the same frequency with which World Series victories eluded them. Campy was paralyzed in a car accident in January 1958; he was 36. Gil Hodges died of a heart attack two days shy of his 48th birthday. Junior Gilliam died at 50. Robinson lost his sight in one eye and was dead by the age of 53, a victim of diabetes. Furillo died at age 66.

Brooklyn fans thought that the magic would last forever. They learned that it was not the alien Yankees who were the enemy, but someone already within the walls—Walter O'Malley, who moved the Dodgers to California and doomed their old ballpark.

"The Boys of Summer" celebrate a first-game victory in the 1952 World Series. Pictured (left to right) *are Joe Black (the winning pitcher), Duke Snider (who hit a two-run homer), manager Charlie Dressen, Pee Wee Reese, and Jackie Robinson.*

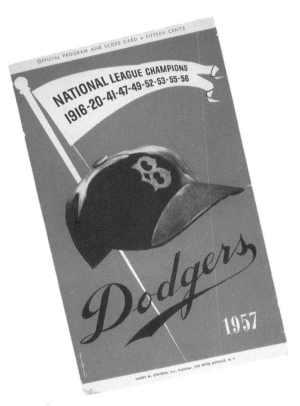

The Dodger program for 1957, the year Brooklyn lost its team.

Most shots, however, caromed off of it in any one of a number of possible and unpredictable directions.

Any team nicknamed "Dem Bums" had to have been colorful, and the Dodgers certainly were. Perhaps the ballclub is best remembered today for breaking baseball's color line, which it did with the signing of Jackie Robinson in 1947, and for the victories of the 1950s. But many Dodger teams down through the years, certainly those of the 1920s and 1930s, reveled in that indefinable quality called "daffiness." And the daffiest Dodger of all had to have been Babe Herman—though Bobo Newsom, Kirby

Johnny Podres (barely visible) is mobbed by his teammates at Yankee Stadium as the Dodgers finally beat their arch-rivals in the 1955 World Series. This Series yielded the Brooklyn team its only world championship. Gil Hodges is number 14, Jim Gilliam 19, Roy Campanella 39, and Jackie Robinson is to the left of Podres. A ticket for the third game of that World Series is seen at right. That day Brooklyn beat the Yankees by a score of 8-3, giving Johnny Podres his first World Series victory.

Higbe, and even manager Wilbert Robinson could have vied for the honor. Brooklyn's Babe was an awesome hitter—he had 1,818 lifetime hits and a career average of .324—but he is best remembered for his bizarre behavior, exemplified by that day in August 1926 when he doubled into a double play. That epic moment came in the seventh inning of a 1-1 game, with one man out and the bases loaded, Herman blasted the ball off the top of the right field fence and raced toward second base. When he got there, he saw a teammate caught in a rundown between third and home. Assuming that the first two runners had scored and that this one would soon be tagged out, Babe lit out for third. He slid in only to discover that another runner was still there, and that a third, having escaped the rundown, had made it back to the overpopulated sack. The bewildered Boston third baseman tagged everybody in sight, which left the umpire to decide who was out and who was not. The result: the most unusual double play in baseball history had occurred where one was most likely to expect it— at the daffy Dodgers' Ebbets Field.

Probably the highlight of Ebbets Field history was the day Jackie Robinson—signed by Branch Rickey—first played there as a Brooklyn Dodger on April 15, 1947. No black player had ever worked in the majors before—not in the 20th century at least. Robinson's contribution to the Dodgers' victory that day was minimal—no hits and a run scored— but his contribution to the game of baseball, to African-Americans in particular, and to the human race in general will live as long as memory endures. No token Negro, Robinson spearheaded the famous "Boys of Summer" team that won six National League pennants and, after so many bitter defeats before the hated Yankees, the 1955 World Series.

Ebbets Field is now a low-rent housing project, named after Jackie, in a decaying section of Brooklyn. But Ebbets Field still lives in the minds of millions of Brooklynites, an imperishable image of glory and independence of spirit. They can still see Robinson at third, Pee Wee Reese at shortstop, Junior Gilliam at second, Gil Hodges making incredible stretches at first, Roy Campanella behind the plate calling signals to Carl Erskine ("Oisk!"), Don Newcombe, Johnny Podres, or Clem Labine. Sandy Amoros is in left, Snider in center, and Furillo anticipating the caroms in right. No one can take that away, nor can they take away the spirit that was, and maybe still is, Brooklyn.

This 1946 photo provides a good view of the sign in which Brooklyn haberdasher, Abe Stark, offered a free suit to any player who could hit the mark. The groundskeeper in the picture is preparing the field for a playoff game between the Dodgers and the Cardinals, who ended the 1946 season in a dead heat.

Perhaps no one epitomized the daffiness of the daffy Brooklyn Dodgers more than Babe Herman, who once doubled into a double play when three runners ended up on third base.

A big crowd watches the opening day ceremonies at Wrigley Field in 1916, the Cubbies's first season in the ballpark.

A Wrigley Field favorite, Hall of Fame catcher Gabby Hartnett played for the Cubs from 1922 until 1940 and saw action in four World Series.

WRIGLEY FIELD

Chicago, Illinois

1914–

Wrigley Field, originally Weegham Park, was built for the Chicago Whales of the Federal League. The Cubs have used the park since 1916.

IN OUR AGE OF EXCESS, Wrigley Field, a spare, simple ballpark on Chicago's North Side, stands out as baseball's most honored shrine. While so many major league teams perform on high-tech, plastic "grass" under magically lighted domes before fans seated in antiseptically clean grandstands, the Chicago Cubs still play ball in an unpretentious, brick-and-concrete park held together by an undisguised steel frame. Until 1988, Wrigley even shunned stadium lights as an intrusion of the modern age on a sport designed to be played in cow pastures.

Wrigley Field, originally Weegham Park, was not built for the beloved Cubbies. In 1914, Charles Weegham, owner of the Chicago Whales of the fledgling Federal League, leased an open lot near the intersection of Addison Road and Clark Street and commissioned Zachary Taylor Davis, who had previously designed Comiskey Park, to build a home for his team. The single-deck, 14,000-seat, V-shaped grandstand with wooden outfield bleachers was completed in time for the opening of the 1914 Federal League season. After two summers, the Federal League folded, but Weegham was able to purchase controlling interest in the National League Chicago Cubs and move that team from its

William Wrigley, Jr., the Chicago chewing-gum maker, purchased the Cubs in 1918 and gave his name to their home field.

home at West Side Grounds to his park for the 1916 season. Two years later, Weegham sold the team to one of his investors, William Wrigley, the Chicago chewing gum manufacturer.

In 1926, Wrigley renamed the park after himself and began to make the renovations that gave Wrigley Field its present appearance. A covered second deck was added to the grandstand, doubling the park's seating capacity. Concrete bleachers were installed during the 1937 season. Two years earlier, the park's most loved adornment—its 75-foot-by-27-foot scoreboard—had been erected above the center field bleachers by the maverick baseball executive, Bill Veeck. Still in use—and still hand-operated—the scoreboard shows inning-by-inning scores of other team's games. In 1937, Veeck also ordered ivy planted near the base of the outfield walls. Those vines, still crawling up their supporting structures, help give Wrigley Field its Ivy League charm.

Wrigley's playing field is, of course, grass, and its dimensions are small. The ivy-covered brick wall in left field is a reasonable 355 feet from home plate, but the power alley in left is only 368 feet. Center field is 400 feet from the batter, the alley in right center is a very reachable 363 feet, and the foul pole in right is 353 feet. Hitters might speak of "the Friendly Confines of Wrigley Field," but to pitchers, the park is an enemy, especially when the Windy City's gusts are blowing out toward center field. On one such occasion, May 17, 1979, the Cubs and the Philadelphia Phillies engaged in a slugfest that made major league history. In 10 innings, the Phils edged the Cubbies, 23-22. The game featured 13 first-inning runs (seven by the Phils and six by the Cubs), 11 home runs, 11 doubles, and 50 hits in all. Eleven pitchers were conscripted in an unsuccessful attempt to stop the madness.

Cub fans are some of baseball's most devoted enthusiasts, but the team has never been able to reward its faithful with a World Series banner to fly above Wrigley's rooftop. The team won pennants in 1918, 1929, 1932, 1935, 1938, and 1945, but every World Series ended in defeat for the Cubs. According to the legend, Babe Ruth delivered the supreme insult to Cub fans during the 1932 Series by reportedly calling a home run at Wrigley Field. After a four-

Wrigley's most charming architectural feature is its ivy-covered outfield wall. Here Cubs' left fielder Ralph Kiner watches a long drive clear the wall for a home run.

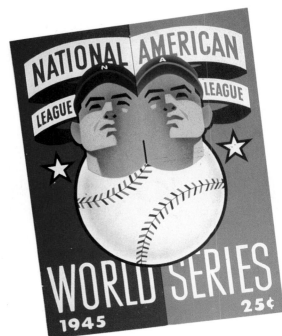

(Left) *The great Grover Cleveland Alexander pitched for the Cubs from 1918 until 1926, twice winning more than 20 games a season.*

(Far left) *This wartime World Series scorecard sold for only a quarter.*

decade drought, Chicago won a divisional title in 1984 and again in 1989, but both times the Cubs were beaten in the National League Championship Series and were unable to advance to the Fall Classic. Many seasons ended in bitter disappointment for the Cub faithful. In 1969, the team had an eight-game lead in August, but the Miracle Mets charged ahead to win the divisional title. In the 1984 National League Championship Series, the Cubs won the first two games and needed only a single victory to reach the World Series, but they lost three straight to the Padres and watched the Series on television.

Despite their failures, the Cubs have employed some of the game's greatest and most charming players. Grover Cleveland Alexander pitched at Wrigley from 1918 through 1926. Gabby Hartnett, the future Hall of Fame catcher, was the backbone of the National League championship teams of the 1930s. The most popular Wrigley performer, however, was Ernie Banks—"Mr. Cub." Besides hitting 512 home runs in 19 Cub seasons, Banks brought to Wrigley Field a youthful zeal that inspired even the last-place teams on which he played. On sunny June afternoons, Mr. Cub would enter the Wrigley Field clubhouse and announce, "Let's play two!" Banks was enshrined in Cooperstown in 1977.

Considering his popularity among Cub fans, it was most appropriate that Banks (along with another popular Cubbie, Billy Williams) was called upon to throw out the first ball for one of Wrigley Field's most historic games. After years of pressure from baseball's rulers and the television networks, the Cubs finally agreed to attach light

Fans swarm Wrigley Field's ticket windows before a big game in this undated photo.

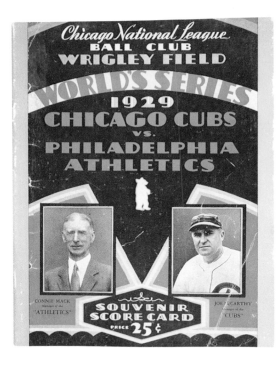

The cover of this 1929 World Series program shows the managers of the two combatants: Connie Mack of the Athletics and Joe McCarthy of the Cubs.

This ticket admitted a fan to game one of the 1929 World Series at Wrigley Field.

The Babe Calls His Shot

The home run that Babe Ruth blasted at Wrigley Field in the fifth inning of the third game of the 1932 World Series is one of the most talked about events in baseball history. Besides being the Babe's last World Series four-bagger, it is the one that helped turn Ruth into a mythic hero, a Paul Bunyan in baseball togs.

The Cub players and fans, stung at the outset of the Series by two defeats at Yankee Stadium, were razzing the Babe unmercifully during the first game at Wrigley Field. When Ruth approached the plate in the fifth inning, the score was 4-4, and Charlie Root was on the mound. Ruth swung through Root's first two pitches, and the crowd roared. The next two serves were wide of the plate, and the fans began to boo the Babe for not taking his cuts.

Reports on what happened next differ. Some say that Ruth pointed toward the Cub dugout as a warning to the bench jockeys. Others maintain that he pointed at Root in defiance. Still others claim that he raised his finger, saying, "It only takes one to hit it." But baseball legend has Babe doing something far more grand than any of these mundane explanations would have it. The myth finds him confidently indicating where he intended to send the next pitch—center field.

Root kicked back and threw and, of course, Ruth blasted the ball over the center field wall, a few feet from the flagpole. Perhaps the great sportswriter Paul Gallico, who saw the game, is the person responsible for history's record of the event for he stated that Ruth "pointed like a duelist to the spot where he expected to send his rapier home." Regardless of what really happened, Gallico's version is the one that survived and today few baseball fans would have it otherwise.

towers to Wrigley's roof for night baseball. (Wrigley had purchased lights after the 1941 season, but on December 8 of that year, the day after the Japanese attacked Pearl Harbor, he donated them to the United States Government to be used in the war effort.) On August 8, 1988, the lights were turned on for an evening game against the Mets. Four innings were played, and then the baseball gods, showing their disapproval, sent thunderstorms upon Wrigley to wash out the contest. The next night, the weather cleared, and the Cubs beat the Mets.

The Cubs have promised to schedule only about 20 night dates per year, which means that most games at Wrigley will continue to be played in sunlight, much to the delight of the Cub faithful. On game day, the crowds swarm the sidewalks around Wrigley as the elevated trains clatter by. The large red sign on the brick facade behind home plate announces the name of the visiting team and the time for the first pitch. Crowds begin to appear on the rooftops of buildings on Waveland Avenue to watch the game over the left field bleachers. During the game, the rowdy bleacher bums roar for the Cubs—and disdainfully toss back onto the field the home run balls hit by Cub opponents. During the seventh-inning stretch, ageless broadcaster Harry Caray leads the crowd in singing "Take Me Out to the Ball Game," and, if all goes well, he shouts out "Cubs win! Cubs win! Cubs win!" at the end of the contest. A white victory flag (blue for a loss) is run up the flagpole, and the fans spill out onto the streets and into the neighborhood bars to discuss their Cubbies. On a sunny June afternoon, fans at Wrigley Field are very close to the heart of baseball.

The legendary sportscaster Harry Caray salutes the camera from his broadcasting booth at Wrigley Field.

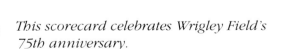

This scorecard celebrates Wrigley Field's 75th anniversary.

Ernie Banks—"Mr. Cub"—played his entire 19-year career with Chicago; he retired with 512 lifetime homers.

Before moving to Braves Field in 1915, the Braves played at South End Grounds. This is a scorecard from their final season there.

This photo shows a crowd gathering outside Braves Field in 1916, the year after the ballpark opened.

BRAVES FIELD
Boston, Massachusetts

1915–1952

A capacity crowd was on hand for the 1948 World Series opener in Braves Field. That day the home team defeated the Cleveland Indians by a score 1-0.

I **N 1912,** when James E. Gaffney bought the National League Boston Braves, most major league teams were playing in stadiums made of concrete and steel, and the remainder were building or planning to build similar edifices to house their clubs. Gaffney's Braves, however, were still working in the miniature South End Grounds, a wooden park on Walpole Street near the railroad lines that led to Providence, Rhode Island and Hartford, Connecticut. Gaffney, obviously envious of his competitors' large modern playing facilities, purchased the Allston Golf Club along Commonwealth Avenue and determined that he would build the grandest baseball arena in the country.

Before commencing his new enterprise, Gaffney did some remodeling on his old park, so construction on Braves Field did not begin until March 20, 1915. On August 18 of that same year, the new arena opened—and the rest of the baseball world was amazed by what Gaffney had wrought. Braves Field had 40,000 seats, making it by far the largest baseball park in the country. A huge, single-deck, covered grandstand wrapped around home plate and up the base lines, and uncovered pavilions were set along

On May 1, 1920, the Braves' Joe Oeschger, shown here, and the Dodgers' Leon Cadore battled in the greatest pitchers' duel in baseball history, a 26-inning 1-1 tie at Braves Field.

The future Yankee slugger, Babe Ruth, began as a pitcher for the Boston Red Sox. While he normally played in Fenway Park, he made an impressive showing at Braves Field in game two of the 1916 Series, beating Dodgers' pitcher Sherry Smith in a riveting, 14-inning affair.

the foul lines in left and right fields. A small section of bleacher seats, called "the Jury Box," was positioned in right field, and a concrete wall ten feet high surrounded the park.

Gaffney was said to be a fan of the inside-the-park home run, and the dimensions of the playing field virtually guaranteed that most home runs would be of that variety. (So did the dead ball that was in use at the time.) The left and right field fences were a distant 402 feet from the batter's box, and the center field wall, 550 feet from home plate, seemed reachable only by trolley. Not surprisingly, it took almost two years for a batter to drive a ball over the outfield wall—Walt Cruise of the Cardinals did it in 1917—though there were plenty of inside-the-park homers to keep Gaffney happy.

The Braves had won the National League pennant and swept the World Series in 1914, the year before they moved to their new park, but in spacious Braves Field they hit poorly and fell from contention. Nonetheless, the park did host the World Series in 1915 and 1916 because the American League champs, the Boston Red Sox, wanted a bigger arena than Fenway Park to host the Fall Classic. That Bosox team was blessed with a talented young southpaw pitcher named Babe Ruth. He had not yet begun to show his prowess at bat, but he had won 18 games on the mound in 1915 and led his team with 23 victories the subsequent summer. Babe had sat out the 1915 World Series as three of

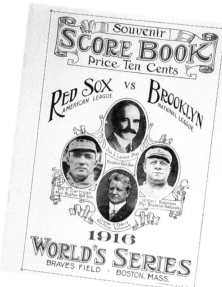

The 1916 World Series featured the Boston Red Sox and the Brooklyn Dodgers, but Boston's home games were played at Braves Field.

1948: The Boston Braves Reach the World Series

During their 38 seasons in Braves Field, the Boston Braves reached the World Series only once, in 1948, when they squared off against a strong Cleveland Indians team.

The Series promised some classic pitching matchups, and fans who appreciated pitchers' duels were not disappointed. In game one, at Braves Field, Johnny Sain, winner of 24 regular-season games, bested the Cleveland ace, Bob Feller, by a score of 1-0, with the two clubs combining for only six hits. In game two, Boston's

Warren Spahn faced Bob Lemon in a duel of future Hall of Famers. This time the Indians triumphed, 4 runs to 1, with Lemon going the distance.

In game three, in Cleveland, the Indians sent 20-game winner Gene Bearden to the mound, and he shut out the Braves on five hits. Sain was ready again for game four, and he pitched superbly, but the Indians beat him, by a score of 2-1, to lead the Series three games to one. The Braves stayed alive with an 11-5 victory in

game five, battering Feller and four other pitchers in the Series' only slugfest.

The Braves' victory in game five brought the Series back to Boston, but Bob Lemon was ready again for the Indians. Though he needed relief help from Bearden in the eighth inning, Lemon was again victorious, edging the hometown Braves with a 4-3 tally. Thus, the Braves' first and last World Series at Braves Field ended in disappointment. They next reached the Fall Classic in 1957, but by that time the club had moved to Milwaukee.

A ticket and scorecard from game six of the 1948 World Series at Braves Field.

his older teammates tamed the Phillies in five games. In the 1916 Series, however, Ruth started the second game at Braves Field and became involved in one of the greatest pitchers' duels in World Series history.

Ruth, opposing Sherry Smith of the Brooklyn Dodgers, allowed an inside-the-park homer to Hy Myers in the first inning, but thereafter he got very stingy, holding the Dodgers in check. Smith allowed the Bosox a run in the third inning and then matched Ruth in a long afternoon of scoreless baseball. At the end of nine innings, the 1-1 score held. Finally, in the 14th inning, Del Gainer, a Boston pinchhitter, delivered a run-scoring single to break the stalemate and give Ruth his first World Series victory. The Red Sox went on to win the Series in five games.

This big park was the home of another famous pitchers' duel a few years later. On May 1, 1920, the Braves' Joe Oeschger and the Dodgers' Leon Cadore battled 26 innings in a 1-1 game that was called a draw after the sun set. In terms of innings, the game is the longest in major league history.

Eventually, the Braves' management sensed that the team's fans were tired of watching pitcher's duels, so, in 1927, wooden fences were placed inside the field's concrete wall to reduce the distance required for a home run. This was the era of Ruth and the power hitter, but no Ruthian hero emerged in a Braves uniform, and the team wallowed in the National League's second division for many seasons. Not even a new manager named Casey Stengel, brought aboard in 1938, could turn the club around. Casey's Braves finished in seventh place four straight times, and attendance dropped sharply.

Finally, after World War II, two

After World War II, two young hurlers, Warren Spahn (left) and Johnny Sain pitched the Braves into championship contention.

pitching sensations, Johnny Sain and Warren Spahn, arrived in Boston and pitched the Braves into contention. The team finished in fourth place in 1946 and rose to third in 1947. Braves' followers began crying "Spahn and Sain, then pray for rain," signaling unwavering faith in Boston's two mound aces and a lack of confidence in the team's third and fourth starters. In 1948, after 33 pennantless seasons, the Braves finally won the National League flag. Spahn and Sain pitched well in the World Series, but Bob Lemon of the Indians emerged as the pitching star, and Cleveland won in six games.

The Braves foundered after that championship season, and attendance dropped again. The crosstown Red Sox had a contending team and a top drawing card in Ted Williams, and the Braves simply failed to pull Beantown fans away from Fenway Park. After a seventh-place finish in 1952, and a home attendance of only 280,000, the Braves bolted for Milwaukee, leaving their former home empty.

A few years later, Braves Field was purchased by nearby Boston University and turned into a football field. Parts of the old park still stand—the first base grandstand, one of the entranceways, and the concrete wall in center and right fields. Baseball traditionalists are undoubtedly glad that the old ballpark is still in use as Nickerson Field, but they would be disappointed to hear that these days the playing area is covered with Astroturf.

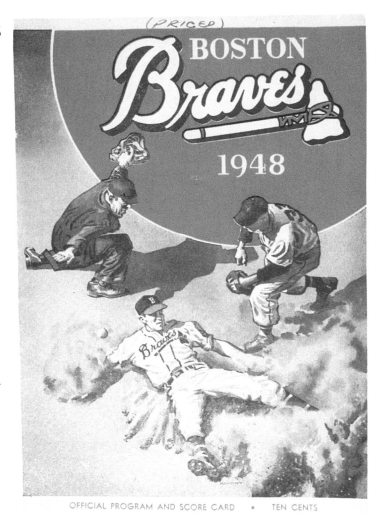

This scorecard sold for only ten cents at Braves Field in 1948.

This photo of Yankee Stadium was taken in 1926, before the triple-tiered grandstand was extended past the foul poles.

This souvenir is from the 1938 World Series, which the Yanks swept in four games against the Cubs.

Pictured here is Babe Ruth belting out his record-setting 60th home run of the season on September 30, 1927, at Yankee Stadium. Blasts like this gave the park its enduring nickname: "the house that Ruth built."

YANKEE STADIUM

Bronx, New York

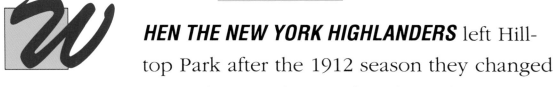

1923–1974, 1976–

The remodeled Yankee Stadium, which opened in 1976, looks like a brand-new ballpark.

WHEN THE NEW YORK HIGHLANDERS left Hilltop Park after the 1912 season they changed their name to the Yankees and moved to the Polo Grounds, the home field of the National League New York Giants. The two teams shared the same park amiably for several seasons, but in 1920, after lease squabbles and other disagreements arose, Charles Stoneham, the Giants' owner, informed the Yanks that he would no longer have them as tenants. In February 1921, the Yankees' owners, Jacob Ruppert and Tillinghast Huston, acquired a large piece of land bordered by 161st Street and River Avenue in the Bronx and began to plan the most impressive baseball arena in the world.

Ruppert and Tillinghast owned a fine team—the Yanks had finished in third place in 1920 and would capture American League flags in 1921 and 1922. They also had the game's best drawing card, Babe Ruth, whose 54 home runs in 1920 had exhilarated the baseball world. The Yankee owners deemed that they needed a grand ballpark to showcase their club, one that would also capture the verve, energy, and excitement of New York City. Construction began in May 1922, and

Casey Stengel was the manager-in-residence at Yankee Stadium from 1949 through 1960, during which time the Bronx Bombers won 10 American League pennants and seven World Series titles.

Yankee Stadium—the first baseball field to be called a stadium—was ready for the opening of the 1923 season.

Yankee Stadium made the other pro teams' parks look like bush league ball yards. It held more that 70,000 patrons, twice the capacity of most other arenas. The seats were arranged in three concrete decks, held in place by steel girders. The grandstand wrapped behind home plate and up the base lines, and wooden bleachers were placed beyond the outfield fences. (Years later, the triple-deck grandstands would be extended beyond the foul poles, and concrete bleachers would be installed.) The outside of the stadium was accented with arch-shaped windows, and the inside of the top deck was lined with a noble facade, which became the arena's most distinguishing feature. Like a large cathedral, Yankee Stadium demanded respect and homage.

The Yanks' new home soon became known as "the house that Ruth built" and the tag was not an exaggeration. Knowing the Babe's powerful left-handed swing, Ruppert and Huston had determined that their park would favor portside swingers. The home run distance down the right field line was only 296 feet, and the adjacent power alley was only 344. The fences in center and left center fields, however, were much friendlier to pitchers, and that section of the field became known as "Death Valley." Only a handful of players in the park's history have belted a ball over the 461-foot sign near the flagpole in dead center field.

During his 13 seasons with the Yanks, Joe DiMaggio batted .325, blasted 361 homers, and patrolled Yankee Stadium's expansive center field with grace and style.

Yankee catcher Yogi Berra bear-hugs Don Larsen after the journeyman pitcher hurled a perfect game in the fifth contest of the 1956 World Series at Yankee Stadium.

Wisely, the Yankee management has usually tried to stock the team with left-handed power hitters. Ruth led the team to a World Series victory in 1923. In 1925, another lefty swinger, Lou Gehrig, became the Yanks' regular first baseman, and the team won eight pennants and seven World Series over the next 15 seasons. During the late 1930s and 1940s, a powerful right-handed hitter named Joe DiMaggio spearheaded the Yankee attack, but a complement of strong lefties—Bill Dickey, Tommy Henrich, Charlie Keller, and Yogi Berra—always surrounded Joltin' Joe to help make the Yanks baseball's most successful franchise. In the 1950s, the switch-hitting Mickey Mantle led the team to eight pennants and in 1960 Roger Maris, whose compact left-handed swing was perfectly suited to the configurations of the stadium, came on board. He and the Mick became known as the feared "M & M boys." In more recent summers, Reggie Jackson, Graig Nettles, and Don Mattingly have provided left-handed firepower. To negate their opponents' left-handed bats, the Yanks have always employed top-notch southpaw pitchers—Herb Pennock, Lefty Gomez, Whitey Ford, Sparky Lyle, Ron Guidry, and Dave Righetti.

Despite the great number of awesome sluggers who have played in the big Bronx ballpark, no major leaguer has ever hit a fair ball that completely left the stadium, al-

One of the most moving moments in Yankee Stadium history took place on July 4, 1939, when Lou Gehrig, the great Yankee first baseman who was dying from the disease that would bear his name, made his farewell speech to his fans, calling himself "the luckiest man on the face of the earth."

The Greatest Football Game Ever Played

Other athletes besides baseballers have tread the sacred Yankee Stadium turf, though today the park is used almost exclusively for baseball. The Stadium has hosted 30 championship boxing fights, including the one on June 22, 1938, when Joe Louis KO'd Max Schmeling in the first round to win the heavyweight title.

On December 28, 1958, the Stadium was also the setting for what has been called the best championship game in National Football League history. The contestants were the hometown New York Giants, with Charlie Conerly, Kyle Rote, and Frank Gifford, and the visiting Colts of Baltimore, whose attack was spearheaded by quarterback John Unitas.

The Colts dominated the first half and led by a score of 14-3 at intermission. But the Giants came back, scoring two second-half touchdowns and holding the Colts scoreless until the game's final moments. Trailing by three points with less than two minutes remaining, Unitas, with precision passes to Raymond Berry, his favorite receiver, drove his team 73 yards to set up the tying field goal. Then, in the first overtime period in regular league competition, Unitas marched his troops 80 yards for the winning touchdown, which was scored when fullback Alan Ameche plunged into the end zone from the Giants' one yard line. Unitas' performance under title-game pressures—completing 26 of 40 passes for 349 yards—ranks with the best in Yankee Stadium history.

Quarterback John Unitas scrambles for 16 yards against the New York Giants in the 1958 NFL title game at Yankee Stadium, a riveting contest won by the Colts in overtime by a score of 23-17.

though Mantle came close. In a 1963 game against the Kansas City Athletics, the Mick blasted a pitch by Bill Fischer off the top of the facade in deep right field. Observers report that the ball was still traveling upward when it ricocheted back toward the field and claim that it would have soared more than 600 feet had its path not been altered. Fans of Negro baseball, however, maintain that the great Josh Gibson once hit a ball over the bleachers in left field and onto the Bronx street.

Since its grand opening 70 years ago, Yankee Stadium has indeed become hallowed ground—the place where Ruth hit his mammoth homers, where Gehrig made his moving farewell speech, where DiMaggio played so gracefully. On this sacred turf, journeyman pitcher Don Larsen pitched a perfect World Series game, and Maris shattered Babe's single-season home run record. Fortunately, in the early 1970s, when the

(Above) *Always boisterous and controversial, Reggie Jackson delighted the Yankee Stadium crowd when he smashed three straight homers in the final game of the 1977 World Series.*

(Right) *The great Yankee teams featured topnotch southpaw pitchers. Whitey Ford, who retired with 236 wins and only 106 defeats, was probably the best of the lot.*

(Below) *Yankee Stadium's Monument Park houses memorials to Miller Huggins, Babe Ruth, and other Yankee greats.*

Hall of Famer Mickey Mantle is about to unleash the powerful swing that accounted for his 536 lifetime homers.

New York Giants football team decided to leave the stadium for open space in New Jersey's Meadowlands, New York City authorities, still remembering the sad days when Ebbets Field and the Polo Grounds were abandoned, approved a grand-scale renovation program for Yankee Stadium.

An hour before the game, fans are already arriving at the big Bronx ballpark.

Closed for two seasons, Yankee Stadium was completely remodeled while the Bronx Bombers played their home games at Shea Stadium in Queens. The steel girders that obstructed viewing were removed, seats were replaced, and modern offices, rest rooms, and scoreboards were installed. The center field monuments, which had once been located in the playing area, were set in a small park behind the center field fence. The new stadium opened for the 1976 season, and the Yanks promptly celebrated the renovation with three straight American League pennants. The most memorable Yankee Stadium highlight in those exciting seasons was provided by Reggie Jackson. In the final game of the 1977 World Series, he smacked three consecutive homers—on three consecutive pitches—to give the Bronx Bombers their first World Championship in 15 seasons.

Today, Yankee Stadium stands out majestically from a ragged Bronx cityscape. On game days, traffic jams the surrounding streets, and the Jerome Avenue el rushes noisily by. Fans swarm the sidewalks and hustle in and out of the souvenir shops and food stands across the street from the stadium. Some people may believe that a Meadowlands parking lot makes a better setting for a ballpark, but the Yanks remain committed to New York. Their current lease runs through 2032.

Manager Al Lopez (left) poses with three of his great pitchers before a game at Yankee Stadium during the pennant-winning 1954 season. From left to right, they are Mike Garcia, Bob Lemon, and Early Wynn.

The bleachers crowd is ready for the home opener in this 1930s photo.

CLEVELAND STADIUM
Cleveland, Ohio

The playing field at Cleveland Stadium, as seen from the press booth.

1932–

7 **O SOME FANS,** Cleveland Stadium is still known as "the Mistake by the Lake." Perhaps there is good reason for that unpleasant sobriquet, for when the winds blow off of nearby Lake Erie in the early spring and late summer, Cleveland Stadium is a miserable setting for a baseball game. Often, too, Indians games become fogged out as air masses descend on the park and make tracking fly balls impossible. After one fog-induced postponement several seasons ago, Dennis "Oil Can" Boyd, the Boston Red Sox pitcher who did not study geography at Harvard, stated, "That's what happens when you build a ballpark next to the ocean." Boyd's geography may have been a bit off, but his logic was sound: building a baseball stadium on a Great Lakes shore was probably a bad idea.

The ballpark was also built too big for baseball. A crowd of 34,000 in cozy Fenway Park can rattle the rafters; the same number in 78,000-seat Cleveland Stadium gets lost behind the steel girders, making it seem as if no one in Cleveland cares whether the Indians win or lose. And the fact that the Indians have not won a pennant since 1954 and have not even finished close since 1959 has not helped matters. Most of the time, the Indians seem to be

Cleveland Stadium is too close to the ocean, according to Red Sox pitcher Dennis "Oil Can" Boyd. He meant Lake Erie, of course.

Hall of Famer Bob Feller was 17 years old when he first pitched in Cleveland Stadium. He had six 20-victory seasons with the Tribe.

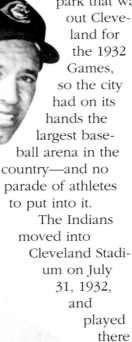

playing in front of relatives and family friends.

The size of Cleveland Public Municipal Stadium can be attributed to the city's desire to draw the 1932 Summer Olympics. It was, in fact, the city of Cleveland and its taxpayers—not the ball club—that paid for the stadium's construction, a scheme of financing that has become the norm for the venues of professional sports. In fact, since Cleveland Stadium was built, Dodger Stadium is the only major league ballpark that was constructed solely with team money. But Los Angeles beat out Cleveland for the 1932 Games, so the city had on its hands the largest baseball arena in the country—and no parade of athletes to put into it.

The Indians moved into Cleveland Stadium on July 31, 1932, and played there through the 1933 season but they disliked the enormous ballpark, so they moved back to their old home, League Park, for the 1934 campaign. For the next six years, the Indians played most of their games in 18,000-seat League Park and reserved Cleveland Stadium for Sundays and holidays, when larger crowds might be expected. In the middle of the 1939 season when lights were added to the larger park, the Indians also scheduled night games at Cleveland Stadium. Only in 1947, after League Park, a brick structure that opened in 1891, literally began to fall apart, did the Indians reluctantly make Cleveland Stadium their sole and permanent home.

Given its rather unfortunate history, perhaps no one will miss this huge, old, double-deck ballpark after 1994, when the Indians are scheduled to move into the $344-million stadium that Cleveland voters approved in a 1990 referendum (after the team's

Larry Doby, shown here in one of his first games at Cleveland Stadium, became the American League's first African-American player in July 1947.

owners threatened to leave town). Then only fans of the Cleveland Browns football team will enter the gateways of the stadium's classic facade. Undoubtedly most Clevelanders will be delighted to watch a baseball game in the warmer, cleaner, and more intimate atmosphere of their new stadium. Perhaps the new park will even inspire the Tribe to a pennant. Nonetheless, Indians fans old enough to remember games at Cleveland Stadium during the late 1940s and early 1950s will have fond memories of that old ball yard on Lake Erie.

From 1942 through 1950, Hall of Famer Lou Boudreau wore two caps for the Indians: he played shortstop, and he managed the team.

The Cleveland Indians' first pennant came in 1920, and it took the club more than 25 years to build another contender. The first sign that the Indians were on the right track came in 1936 with the arrival of a 17-year-old, right-handed pitcher from Van Meter, Iowa: Bobby Feller. Used sparingly during his first two seasons, Feller worked his way into the Indians' rotation in 1938, won 17 games, and led the American League with 240 strikeouts. During the next three seasons, Feller won 24, 27, and 25 games and led the loop in strikeouts each year. By then, he was known as "Rapid Robert," the hardest thrower since Walter Johnson. World War II interrupted Feller's career, but he returned to action in 1946, won 26 times that season, and struck out a record 348 batters.

Be-

This shot of Cleveland Stadium shows its proximity to Lake Erie.

fore World War II, Cleveland Stadium had been a pitcher's park, with a monstrous center field lawn. In 1947, when the Indians moved in for good, a fence was erected in front of the outfield walls to make the park more favorable to Joe Gordon and other big hitters. It was then 321 feet at the foul lines, 365 feet in the power alleys, and 410 feet to straightaway center. (In 1991, the fences were moved deeper.) Nonetheless, shortstop-manager Lou Boudreau built his team around solid starting pitchers: Feller, Bob Lemon, and Gene Bearden. In 1948, Feller won 19 games and Lemon and Bearden won 20 apiece, leading the Indians to

their first American League pennant in 28 seasons. In the World Series, Indian pitchers held the Boston Braves to only three runs in the first four contests; Cleveland won the Series in six games, the team's first and only World Championship.

In 1949, Bearden failed to repeat his previous year's success, but Mike Garcia and Early Wynn were added to Cleveland's rotation, forming, along with Feller and Lemon, "the Big Four" that would keep the Indians in contention for several seasons. When the Yankees visited Cleveland during those great summers, crowds of 75,000 or more swarmed into Cleveland Stadium to watch the Tribe's Big Four take on the talented Yankee moundsmen: Whitey Ford, Eddie Lopat, Allie Reynolds, Vic Raschi. On one such occasion, a doubleheader on September 12, 1954, 84,587 fans jammed Cleveland Stadium—an American League regular-season attendance record that still stands. That season, the Indians won the pennant, finishing with a magnificent 111-43 record, a feat undiminished by the team's four-game World Series loss to Willie Mays' New York Giants.

One other noteworthy event occurred in Cleveland Stadium during those great Indian summers: on July 5, 1947, Bill Veeck, the team's progressive owner, signed Larry Doby to a major league contract. Doby was the second African-American player to appear in a major league game and the first black American Leaguer. Though he never reached the heights of his predecessor, Jackie Robinson, Doby played 13 solid major league seasons with a grace and dignity that helped clear a path for other black players.

When the Indians begin to play in their new park some time during the 1994 season, many of their fans will want to forget Cleveland Stadium and the losing teams that have occupied it over the last four decades. Older fans with longer memories, however, will know that the old park once housed some pretty fair teams—and some terrific pitchers.

In another of the great publicity stunts for which he was famous, Indians' president Bill Veeck presided over a burial service for the team's 1948 championship flag before a game on September 23, 1949, at Cleveland Stadium. The programs for the 1948 Series and season are shown above left and right, respectively, and a ticket for game three of the Series is at left.

He Came Second: Larry Doby

In April 1947, when Jackie Robinson was making baseball and civil rights history with the Brooklyn Dodgers, Larry Doby was playing for the Negro League's Newark Eagles. A schoolboy star at East Side High in Paterson, New Jersey, Doby, at age 22, was already one of his league's top players. In 1947, while all African-American baseball fans were following the achievements of Robinson, Doby was tearing up the Negro League with a .400 average.

Bill Veeck, the Cleveland Indians' owner, had been watching Doby for some time. He wanted to sign the young Negro League star with little fanfare so that Doby would not feel the same pressures that Robinson faced as he traveled around the league. "One afternoon when the team trots out on the field, a Negro player will be out there with them," Veeck casually told a black newspaper reporter early in the 1947 season.

On July 5 of that year, Veeck purchased Doby's contract from Newark for $10,000. Three hours later, Doby was approaching home plate as a Cleveland Indian pinch hitter in a game against the White Sox at Comiskey Park.

Like many other nervous rookies, Doby struck out in his first major league at bat. Used sparingly in 1947, he batted only .156, yet he was well received by the hometown fans. The next season, Doby became a starter and batted .301 in Cleveland's pennant-winning campaign. He hit .318 in the World Series and became the first African-American player to hit a Series home run; his third-inning homer at Cleveland Stadium in game four was the difference in the Indians' 2-1 victory.

In his 13 major league seasons, Doby won two home run crowns and an RBI title. He retired with 253 lifetime homers and a .283 batting average.

The Indians first played at Cleveland Stadium in 1932, but it did not become their permanent home until 1947.

The tables are set for a pre-game meal at Cleveland Stadium's restaurant, where photos on the walls capture great moments in Indians' and Browns' history.

C O U N T Y
STADIUM

Milwaukee, Wisconsin

BEFORE 1953, the shape of the baseball world, like the diamond itself, was a given: there were two leagues of eight teams, all playing in the cities that had been their homes since the beginning of the century or earlier. But after the 1952 season, the Boston Braves, deeming that Beantown could not support two major league teams, decided to move on. They chose Milwaukee, which was close enough to the other National League teams to preclude travel problems in the pre-jet age but far enough away from rival cities to avoid dividing the loyalties of the local fans. The world of baseball has never been the same.

Other franchise shifts followed in short order. Before the decade was over, the St. Louis Browns had moved to Baltimore, becoming the Orioles, and the Dodgers and Giants had decamped for California. Soon to follow were the Philadelphia Athletics, who went first to Kansas City and then to Oakland, and the Washington Senators who moved to Minneapolis-St. Paul where they were rechristened the Twins. (Washington then got a replacement team, which subsequently stole off to Texas to become the Rangers.)

In this aerial view, County Stadium is a green expanse in a sea of parking lots. The park hosted the Milwaukee Braves from 1954 through 1965 and the Brewers from 1970 through the present.

Although Milwaukee had no major league team in 1970, when this photo was taken, County Stadium was still well kept. At the time, the city was hoping to lure the old Seattle Pilots to Wisconsin.

(Opposite) Robin Yount won the American League's Most Valuable Player Award in 1982, with a batting average of .331, 29 homers, and 114 RBI's.

Harvey Haddix is congratulated by manager Danny Murtaugh as he walks off the County Stadium mound on May 26, 1957. The shellshocked look on Haddix's face may reflect his loss in the 13th inning, after pitching 12 perfect frames.

Ironically, Milwaukee, the first beneficiary of the wanderlust, held its franchise for only 13 seasons, from 1953 through 1965, when low attendance and the drawing power of the burgeoning South lured the Braves to Atlanta. For two years, 1968 and 1969, the White Sox played a very limited schedule of games in County Stadium, and then, in 1970, the expansionist Seattle Pilots, which vied with Cleveland for the dubious honor of being the league's worst team and, hence, could not draw in its first season in the Pacific Northwest, scurried off to Milwaukee to become the Brewers.

County Stadium, which played host to both the Braves and the Brewers, is pleasing if unspectacular. It holds about 53,000 fans in a double-deck grandstand that engulfs the field and two sections of benched bleachers separated by the bullpens in straightaway center field. Behind the bleachers is the scoreboard, a rather plain affair adorned with only an analog clock and the Brewers' logo (an *m* with an angled *b* beneath it to form what looks like a baseball mitt with a ball filling the empty space within the *b*). Above and below the scoreboard are advertisements. At one time, an enormous beer keg and a small shack were mounted near the scoreboard and, after a Brewer homer, "Bernie Brewer" would slide down from his shack into the barrel. Distances to the outfield fences are moderate: 315 feet to left field, 362 feet to the power alleys, 397 feet to the deep alleys, 402 feet to center field, and precisely 315.37 feet to the right field foul pole.

When the Braves first moved to Milwaukee, enthusiasm for major league baseball's arrival in Wisconsin was almost palpable. In his novel Shoeless Joe, W. P. Kinsella writes of Milwaukee fans who, after hearing that their city would get a major league baseball franchise, assembled at County Stadium "and smiled out at the empty playing field—sat in silence, in awe, in wonder, in anticipation, in joy—just knowing that soon the field would come alive with the chatter of infielders, bright as bird chirps." Sold-out games were the norm. After struggling in Boston to garner any enthusiasm, the Braves must have felt as though they had reached baseball's pearly gates. And they played better too. After winning the 1948 pennant in Boston, the Braves had dropped in the standings. In their new home, they jumped to second place in 1953, fell to third the next year, and then returned to second in 1955 and 1956. They copped the Na-

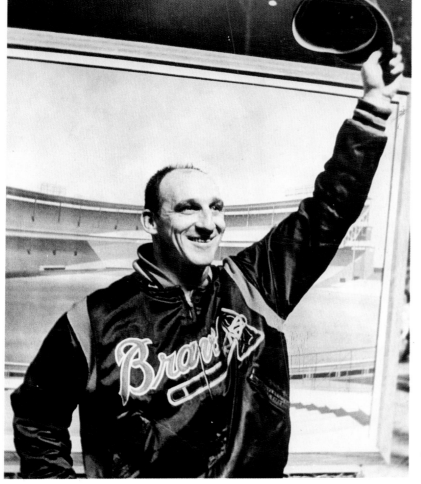

Warren Spahn acknowledged the cheers of 34,000 fans on September 17, 1963, the night that he was honored at County Stadium. Among other gifts, he received a painting of the ballpark, which is behind him in this photo.

tional League pennant in 1957 and again in 1958. They won the World Series in their first attempt by beating the powerful Yankees in seven games. The next year, the New Yorkers avenged their loss by the same margin, becoming the first team since 1925 to win the Series after being down three games to one.

After the successes of 1957 and 1958, the Braves looked as if they had the makings of a Milwaukee dynasty, but that was not the case. They finished in second place in 1959 and 1960, and then slid to the middle of the pack. With their declining fortunes on the field came declining local interest and attendance. Whereas County Stadium had once been filled with fans, the echoes of bats and balls could now be heard in the land of empty seats. For the second time in their history, the Braves moved— this time to Atlanta, where, in their first season, they finished in fifth place.

For a few years, County Stadium was dark. The Chisox night games scheduled there in 1968 and 1969 were a sort of test: if fans showed up, Milwaukee might get another major league team. The audition went well, so in 1970 the Brewers (née Pilots) moved in. Their performance has been spotty but, burned by the Braves' defection, Milwaukee fans have remained loyal. In 1982, their loyalty paid off when manager Harvey Kuenn led a motley crew—nicknamed "Harvey's Wallbangers"—to the American League pennant. But in the "Suds Series" against the Cardinals of Busch Stadium, Harvey's nine could not prevail and lost in seven games.

Milwaukee's best players during the past almost 40 years are not hard to spot; two pitchers and two batters easily take the honors. Lew Burdette, who came to the Braves in a trade that sent Johnny Sain to the Yankees, won 173 games while pitching for Milwaukee, and almost single-handedly destroyed the Bronx Bombers with his three victories in the 1957 World Series. And

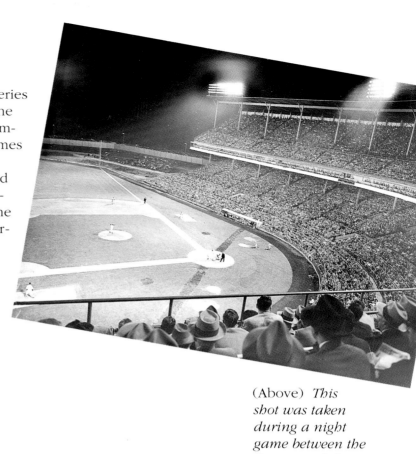

(Above) *This shot was taken during a night game between the Braves and the Chicago Cubs in 1953, Milwaukee's first year of major league baseball.*

(Left) *Lew Burdette, who came to the Braves in a trade that sent Johnny Sain to the Yankees, won 173 games while pitching for Milwaukee. He almost single-handedly destroyed the Bronx Bombers with his three victories in the 1957 World Series.*

Hank Aaron's 109th Home Run

Everyone remembers Hank Aaron's 715th lifetime homer. Hit in Atlanta on April 8, 1974, while a national television audience watched, it broke Babe Ruth's "unbreakable" career home run record. Aaron has always maintained, however, that his 109th homer, hit in County Stadium on September 23, 1957, gave him just as great a thrill.

It came at the end of a tough pennant race between Aaron's Milwaukee Braves and Stan Musial's St. Louis Cardinals. In late September, the Braves had pulled ahead of the Redbirds, mounting a five-game lead with only six contests left to play. On a Monday night, the Cards came to Milwaukee hoping to sweep a three-game series and get back into the race.

Monday night's game was a tight one. Three Cardinal pitchers dueled Milwaukee's Lew Burdette into the 11th inning. The score was tied 2-2, one Brave was on base, and two men were out when Aaron approached the plate in the home half of the 11th inning. A young reliever named Billy Muffett threw Aaron a slow curve ball, and Aaron swung for the fences. When Hank connected, the ball traveled on a long arc toward the center field fence, clearing the barrier with plenty to spare. The Braves' 4-2 victory clinched the pennant for Milwaukee, and Aaron was carried off the field by his jubilant teammates.

The homer was Aaron's 43rd of the year. He would finish the regular season with one more plus a league-leading 132 RBIs and a .322 average—a report card that earned him the Most Valuable Player Award. And led by Aaron's .393 average and three homers, the Braves went on to upset the New York Yankees in the World Series.

Mustachioed Rollie Fingers pours champagne on the head of manager Harvey Kuenn after the Brewers clinched the American League Eastern Division title in 1982. A ticket from game three of the ensuing World Series is at right.

Warren Spahn played with the Boston and Milwaukee Braves from 1942 through 1964, winning 20 or more games nine times while the team played at County Stadium.

As for the hitters, two names stand out. Hank Aaron began and ended his career at County Stadium. He broke into the majors with the Braves in 1954 and played his final two seasons, 1975 and 1976, with the Brewers. Playing for Milwaukee teams, he hit 420 of his 755 career homers. The other great County Stadium player of note is the current Brewers' star, Robin Yount, whose hitting and fielding with the team since 1974 should assure him a spot in Cooperstown when his remarkable career ends.

Not only local favorites have performed well at County Stadium. Old-timers probably remember the day in 1961 when Willie Mays blasted four homers in a single game, or the time two years later when Harvey Haddix of the Pirates pitched 12 perfect innings and lost in the 13th inning on an unearned run.

Whether the home teams have excelled there or not, County Stadium is a nice place in which to see a baseball game. It lacks the glitz and glamour of other parks, but the fans are polite, the sight lines are good, the food is ethnic (bratwurst), and the grass is real. It offers old-fashioned midwestern simplicity—a cold brew in one hand, a sausage in the other, and a good baseball companion at your side. As the ad executive put it, "It doesn't  get any better than this." Nonetheless, Wisconsin Governor Tommy Thompson has just made the first financial moves to create a new stadium for the Brewers, so this pleasant park's days are probably numbered.

Fans are jubilant after game five of the 1982 World Series at County Stadium. At that point in the Series, the Brewers were ahead three games to two, but the Red Birds would win the final two games and take the world championship.

A ticket for game six of the 1957 World Series, in which the Braves lost to the Yanks by a score of 12–3.

A scorecard from the Giant's inaugural season at Candlestick shows the open-ended outfield that was responsible for a great deal of the wind-blown chaos in the ballpark.

Young fans, decked out in their Giants caps, eagerly await a glimpse of their heroes before a game at Candlestick.

On October 28, 1958, Giants' owner Horace Stoneham tamped down the first ceremonial pouring of concrete for what would become Candlestick Park.

CANDLESTICK PARK
San Francisco, California

1960–

Candlestick's grassy field is shown before the players arrive for their pre-game workout.

CANDLESTICK PARK has been called "the Stick" by its loyalists and "the Wind Tunnel" and "the Cave of Winds" by its critics. Perhaps it should be called "the Oy Vay on the Bay," for next to Cleveland's Municipal Stadium, it is probably the worst situated ballpark in the majors. Still, it has endured longer than any stadium in the National League, and the only older National League park still in operation is venerable Wrigley Field. Enclosing center field has helped reduce the wind, but the cold and fog are perpetual problems. Given the weather conditions here, Candlestick Park hosts more daytime games than at any other ballpark, again with the exception of Wrigley Field. How cold and windy is it? Candlestick is the only open-air park with heaters under its 20,000 reserved seats. And it is the only park in the nation where a balk has been called because a pitcher was blown off of the mound (Stu Miller during the first of the two 1961 All-Star Games).

In 1958, when the Giants absconded from New York, they were part of a joint venture. Walter O' Malley wanted to move his Dodgers to the Golden West, but he needed to find another team willing to go to California with him so that other teams could schedule a sufficient number of

The ticket booths are empty, but some 59,000 loyal Giants fans can pack Candlestick Park for a big game.

Pacific Coast games per trip to justify the time and expense of travel in the pre-jet age. Horace Stoneham, whose New York Giants were not doing well either in the standings or at the gate, was induced to follow O'Malley. The Dodgers got warm, sunny Los Angeles, the Giants cultured but cold San Francisco.

During their first two years out West, the Giants played in a magnificent downtown minor league facility called Seals Stadium. This park, built in 1931, had major league dimensions: left field was 340 feet from home plate, center field was 400 feet away, and right field was 365 feet. And though Seals Stadium had only 22,900 seats, the Giants' attendance record in their first two years in California was greater by 587,000 tickets than the total of their previous three seasons in the Polo Grounds.

Perhaps the Giants should have stayed put, but as an inducement to come west, San Francisco's mayor, George Christopher, had promised to build the team a new facility. In 1954, voters approved a $5-million bond issue contingent on a team's moving to the city, and construction began on donated land in August 1958. Then the problems began. Neighbors opposed widening local streets to accommodate traffic that they did not want in the first place. Two grand juries investigated irregularities in funding the stadium (though no indictments were handed down). The Teamsters struck the project, preventing the installation of seats. In November 1959, Stoneham called the infield "unplayable," and a new one had to be installed. And two months later, fire marshals declared the premises a firetrap.

Despite the problems, Candlestick Park opened on April 12, 1960, with 42,269 fans packing the new facility to give a standing ovation to Mrs. John McGraw, widow of the great Giants manager of the first third of the century. The Giants completed the

Regardless of which way Candlestick's winds blew, Willie Mays' drives found the bleachers seats. Mays, shown above, hit 40 homers in 1961, 49 in 1962, 47 two years later, and a career-high of 52 in 1965. Like Mays, Willie McCovey (right), seen here blasting one out of Candlestick in the second game of the 1962 World Series against the Yankees, was undeterred by the park's deep fences and strong winds.

festivities by beating the St. Louis Cardinals by a score of 3-1. Of course, it was the great Willie Mays who brought home all of the Giants' runs—with a first-inning triple and a single in the third. The third inning also saw an unusual delay of game when the umpires noticed something wrong with the foul poles—they were in fair territory, on the playing field itself. Quickly a new ground rule was announced: balls hitting a pole and caroming into the seats would be ground-rule doubles. The poles were subsequently repositioned.

As originally configured in 1960, Candlestick Park could seat 45,774 people. The left field foul pole was 330 feet from home plate, the power alleys were 397 feet, cen-

High on the list of magnificent mounds-men who thrilled Candlestick fans was Hall of Famer Juan Maricial—he won 20 games six times during his 14 San Francisco seasons.

ter field was 420 feet, and right field was 335 feet. This arrangement was deemed unfair, and rightly so, because the park acted as a wind tunnel, funnelling the wind in from left center and out to right center, giving left-handed hitters a decided edge. In 1961, the situation was rectified by shortening the distance to the left center field fence and reducing the dimensions in right center to 375 feet.

But neither deep fences nor strong winds could prevent Mays' drives from reaching the outfield seats. He hit 40 homers in 1961, 49 in 1962, 47 two years later, and a career-high of 52 in 1965. In 1962, he led the Giants to the National League pennant, but his club suffered a seven-game World Series loss to the Yankees, with the final game, which was played at Candlestick, ending in a score of 1-0 when Willie McCovey lined out hard to second baseman Bobby Richardson with the tying and winning runs aboard.

McCovey, like Mays, found Candlestick's seats reachable. Three times he led the National League in homers, and he blasted a total of 521 round-trippers in his Hall of Fame career. Giant sluggers of more recent vintage—Will Clark, Kevin Mitchell, and Matt Williams—have continued the tradition begun by Mays and McCovey. Nonetheless, Candlestick fans have also witnessed some magnificent moundsmen, the two most noteworthy being Hall of Famers Juan Maricial and Gaylord Perry. Maricial won 20 games six times during his 14 San Francisco seasons, and Perry, the notorious spitballer, won nearly half of his 314 lifetime victories while playing for the Giants.

In 1970, Candlestick was revamped so that it could also serve as a home for the National Football League's 49ers. The stadium was fully enclosed, both to reduce the wind and to increase the seating capacity, and Astroturf replaced the natural grass (though turf was put back before the 1979 season). With the new center field seats,

World Series Earthquake

andlestick Park has taken a lot of abuse, most of it deserved, but on the evening of October 17, 1989, it showed what it was made of and helped America put the relationship between sports and "the real world" in perspective.

That night, at 5:03 Pacific Time, televisions across the United States were on, and fans were listening to pre-game chatter, waiting for the start of game three of the World Series at Candlestick Park. In the San Francisco Bay area, it was rush hour, but traffic on the Nimitz Freeway and on the Bay Bridge was much lighter than usual. Most people had left work early to catch the game live or on television.

Then, suddenly, at 5:04, ABC's Al Michaels, in a most uncharacteristic tone of voice, shouted, "We're having an earthq—," and the lines went dead. Emergency generators were quickly activated, and fans across the country could first hear and then see what was happening at Candelstick and around the Bay area. The earthquake had lasted only 30 seconds, but the damage was considerable. The Marina Section of the city was ablaze from ruptured gas lines. Parts of the Nimitz Freeway had collapsed, crushing cars on the lower deck under tons of concrete. A section of the upper span of the Bay

SUITE SEAT
13   1

CANDLESTICK PARK
LUXURY SUITE

Est.Price $49.50
Stad.Opr.Tax.....50
Total .:.....$50.00

GAME 5

1989 WORLD SERIES

GIANTS

VS.
AMERICAN LEAGUE
CHAMPIONS

1989 World Series

THE FALL CLASSIC™

RAIN CHECK subject to the conditions set forth on back hereof
DO NOT DETACH THIS COUPON
A. BARTLETT GIAMATTI
Commissioner of Baseball

CANDLESTICK PARK
LUXURY SUITE

Est.Price $49.50
Stad.Opr.Tax.....50
Total $50.00

GAME 5

1989 WORLD SERIES
13   1
SUITE SEAT

Bridge had fallen onto the lower level, the unbroken macadam having become a slide of death for drivers unable to apply the brakes in time.

At Candlestick, fear, not panic, reigned. People around America watched in fascinated horror as the fans in the park filed out calmly, hoping that the stadium would not come down around them. Wives and children of players came on the field to be comforted by husbands and fathers, no longer just ballplayers but suddenly people with more to lose than a game. Despite understandable apprehension, Candlestick did not collapse. There was some damage, but work crews patched up the weak spots within a few days.

What was to be done about the Series? Down two games to none,

the Giants had hoped to recoup their fortunes back home at Candlestick. But given the damage done by the quake, people wondered if playing the remaining games was the proper thing to do. Baseball Commissioner Fay Vincent, on the job only since the death of his friend and predecessor, Bart Giamatti, two months before, announced his priorities. The concerns of the Bay Area, home to both Series contenders, would come first; the World Series was, after all, merely "our modest little sporting event."

Most fans probably knew that, but it took the awful night of October 17, 1989 and the wisdom of Fay Vincent to remind them. The Series was resumed 12 days later and was won by the A's.

(Above) *This was the scene in Candlestick moments after the earthquake on October 17, 1989. This ticket for the fifth game of that World Series was never used. The A's wrapped up the championship in four outings.*

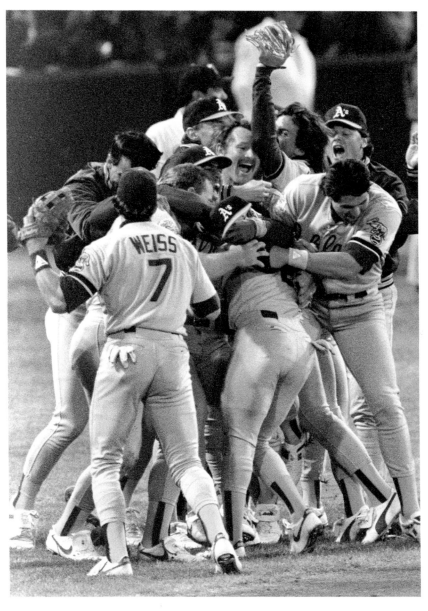

Candlestick could accommodate up to 59,091 baseball fans, making it the largest park in the National League.

But trouble was still brewing for the facility. The renovations had cost $16 million of taxpayers' money, and, adding insult to injury, fans had to pay a surcharge on their tickets. Attendance had been dropping since 1968 when the Athletics arrived across the bay in Oakland. Moreover, during the early 1970s, the A's had a powerhouse team while the Giants were oscillating between mediocre and awful.

The competition from Oakland as well as the winds and cold conspired to reduce attendance so that in 1974 only 520,081 fans passed through the turnstiles, the Giants' lowest attendance record since 1943. Ever since, there has been talk of moving the Giants again—either to another city (Denver, Colorado and Santa Clara, California have often been mentioned) or to a new site in San Francisco. But even in the Golden West, neither the streets nor the wallets of citizens are lined with gold, and local taxpayers have shown a healthy displeasure at the thought of digging deeply into their pockets to build a publicly financed home for a privately owned sports franchise. So it looks as though Candlestick Park is safe, at least for a while. The winds still blow, the fog still rolls in, and the cold is still intense, but economics, that old bugaboo of older parks, might just save this venerable, problem-ridden field for another generation.

The Giants' cross-bay rivals, the Oakland A's, won all four games of the earthquake-interrupted 1989 World Series. Here they celebrate in Candlestick Park after copping the championship.

Candlestick Park's proximity to San Francisco Bay has frequently meant the stadium is plagued with fog and wind, not the ideal conditions for a ballgame. This photo shows just how close the stadium is to the bay.

A scorecard from 1962, the Dodgers' first season at Dodger Stadium.

Manager Tom Lasorda hugs the great Dodger southpaw, Fernando Valenzuela, after the Mexican-born hurler's victory gives Los Angeles the 1981 National League pennant.

DODGER STADIUM
Los Angeles, California

During their first four seasons in Los Angeles, the Dodgers played at the coliseum. This overhead shot shows that the old football arena was ill-suited to the configurations of the summer game.

1962–

HEN THE DODGERS LEFT BROOKLYN for California after the 1957 season, they took up temporary residence in the Los Angeles Coliseum, an oversized football stadium built in the early 1920s and enlarged to host the 1932 Summer Olympics. The 93,000-seat arena was ill-suited for baseball and in no way resembled cozy Ebbets Field, where the Dodgers had spent the previous 45 summers. The playing field was oval, the right shape for a gridiron or quarter-mile track but awkward for the imposition of a baseball diamond. Though the conditions were far from perfect, temporary fencing allowed for a makeshift, oddly shaped baseball field at one end of the arena. The left field wall was a mere 250 feet from home plate—Babe Ruth League distance. It was topped with a 40-foot screen which lacked the charm of Fenway Park's majestic left field barrier. Center and right fields, however, were set at almost unreachable distances. The result was that the Dodgers' first season in the Coliseum saw 182 homers hit to left field while only 11 were directed toward center and right.

No one liked the Coliseum, though the Dodgers won a pennant and the World Series there in 1959. But the old

This shot of the Dodger Stadium scoreboard and the surrounding hills shows the park's placement at the bottom of Chavez Ravine.

Hard-hitting Steve Garvey played a key role on pennant-winning Dodger teams in 1974, 1977, 1978, and 1981.

Although there are no lines at the ticket booths in this photo, the Dodgers consistently lead the National League in home attendance.

football stadium was meant to be only a temporary home while Walter O'Malley, the Dodgers' owner, shopped for a piece of real estate on which to build a new ballpark. He settled on an uneven tract of land called Chavez Ravine. On June 3, 1958, Los Angeles voters approved construction of the new ball field and work began shortly thereafter—but not before a local resident, Manuel Arechiga, his wife, and four granddaughters valiantly fought eviction. The deputies who finally removed the battling Arechiga family suffered bruises as well as bite wounds.

The new ball park, called Dodger Stadium, opened for the 1962 season and is still considered one of the best places in the world to play baseball. Built with 21,000 pre-cast concrete blocks, the 56,000-seat arena resembles in layout some of the classic ballparks of yesteryear, but it has all the amenities of a modern stadium. Its terraced, five-level parking lots hold 16,000 cars and its four decks of uncovered grandstand seats are unencumbered by the steel girders that ruined the sight lines in many of the old parks. With its plain outer facade, Dodger Stadium is both classy and efficient in appearance. Indeed, in few ballparks are the stands cleaner, the aisles roomier, or the seats more comfortable. Not surprisingly, the Dodgers for many years led the majors in home attendance; it was the first team to draw three million fans in a season. The home attendance record of 3,608,881, set in 1982, was broken only after the Toronto Blue Jays moved into their new, retractable-dome stadium in 1989, but the Dodgers still average more than 40,000 fans per game.

Dodger Stadium's playing field is a pitcher's paradise. The foul poles are 330 feet from home plate, and the power alleys,

Hall of Famer Sandy Koufax, shown here pitching in the 1965 World Series, was almost unbeatable in pitcher-friendly Dodger Stadium.

originally set at 380 feet, are now 385. Center field, once 410 feet, is now 400. Although the Los Angeles Dodgers have had a generous share of fence busters in their lineup—the 1977 club was the first in history to feature four players who hit 30 or more homers—Dodger Stadium has generally been kinder to pitchers than hitters.

The first Dodger hurler to profit from the park's dimensions was Sandy Koufax. For his first six seasons with the team, three at Ebbets Field and three in the Coliseum, the Brooklyn-born southpaw had a lifetime 36-40 record, hardly the marks of a future Hall of Famer. In his last season of work at the Coliseum, however, he straightened out, posting an 18-13 record with a league-leading 269 strikeouts. At age 26, he looked as though he would develop into a solid starting pitcher.

The 30-year-old stadium, simple yet elegant in design, still looks like a brand-new ballpark.

But when the Dodgers moved to Chavez Ravine, Koufax's career surpassed all expectations. Instead of pitching with a fence 200 feet behind his right shoulder, he was now working in a stadium where home runs had to travel a considerable distance. In 1962, he finished 25-5 with a 1.88 ERA and 306 strikeouts, marks good enough to earn him both the Cy Young and Most Valuable Player awards. Koufax was an outstanding pitcher in any ballpark, but at Dodger Stadium he was nearly unbeatable. His lifetime mark there, including post-season games, was 63-14.

Like most of the great ones, Koufax performed best in the big games. After winning game one of the 1963 World Series in New York (he fanned a record 15 Yankees), Sandy earned a Series sweep for the Dodgers with a 2-1 six-hit victory over Whitey Ford in game four at Dodger Stadium. Two years later, Koufax lost game two of the Series in Minnesota, then shut out the Twins at Dodger Stadium in game five. He copped the Series for the Dodgers with a three-hit shutout two days later in Minnesota.

Koufax's Dodger teams and their stadium were well matched. Besides Sandy, the pitch-ing staff featured Don Drysdale (another future Hall of Famer), Johnny Podres, and Claude Osteen. Playing in the big park, the offense eschewed the home run in favor of the brand of baseball associated with players of the Ty Cobb era. Maury Wills, the plucky Dodger shortstop, for example, would slap a single, then steal second base. The next hitter would move Wills along with a bunt or a ground ball. Tommy or Willie Davis would then send Wills home with a hit or a long fly.

Unlike the power-hitting Ebbets Field teams, the Dodgers of the 1960s relied on speed to score runs. Here, quick-footed Maury Wills slides home with a run in the fifth game of the 1965 World Series.

Loathed in Brooklyn, Loved in L.A.: Walter O'Malley

The man who broke the hearts of Brooklyn's baseball fans was Walter O'Malley, a Bronx-born attorney whose career with the Dodger front office began in 1930, when he was named to the team's Board of Directors. In 1943, O'Malley, who had been running his own engineering firm in New York, joined the Dodgers on a full-time basis as the team's legal representative. Shortly thereafter, he, John L. Smith, and Branch Rickey, the team's president, bought controlling interest in the club. In 1950, O'Malley purchased Rickey's stock and assumed the title of president.

With O'Malley at the helm, the Brooklyn Dodgers achieved their greatest successes. The famous "Boys of Summer" team won National League pennants in 1952, 1953, 1955, and 1956. The first two of O'Malley's pennant winners fell to the New York Yankees in the World Series, but in 1955 the Dodgers broke the Bronx jinx and won the Series in seven games.

As early as 1953, O'Malley was

telling the public of plans to replace Ebbets Field with a state-of-the-art stadium somewhere in New York City. Even as late as 1957, he still claimed to be negotiating with the city for a new ballpark. After the 1957 season, however, O'Malley took his team west. In California, he made millions; in the process, he became the personal enemy of any Brooklynite who had ever spent a sunny afternoon at Ebbets Field. Today, 35 years after the Dodgers' departure, anti-O'Malley feeling still runs strong in the borough of Brooklyn.

O'Malley died in August 1979, at age 75. The previous season, he saw his Los Angeles Dodgers draw more than three million people, the first time a team had reached that attendance mark.

Walter O'Malley reviews the Los Angeles Coliseum as a potential home for his Dodgers. His move to the West Coast made him wealthy, but it broke the hearts of Brooklyn's baseball fans.

In contrast to the fine Dodger teams of the 1960s, those of the 1970s were more likely to use the long ball as an offensive weapon. Steve Garvey, Ron Cey, Dusty Baker, and the other mainstays of those seasons could reach the fences, but the team still relied on pitchers like Don Sutton, Tommy John, and Burt Hooten to keep their opponents in check. The World Championship teams of 1981 and 1988 were also built around great moundsmen. In 1981, Mexican-born Fernando Valenzuela was the ace. In 1988, Orel Hershiser won 23 games, pitched a record 59 consecutive scoreless innings, and beat the powerful Oakland Athletics twice in the World Series.

A ticket for the inaugural game at Dodger Stadium, which was played on April 10, 1962.

Orel Hershiser, shown here hurling one of his September shutouts in 1988, is one of a number of Dodger pitchers who found their home park very much to their liking.

The accomplishments of Valenzuela and Hershiser notwithstanding, the greatest Dodger Stadium event for today's fans was a home run struck by Kirk Gibson in game one of the 1988 Series. With two outs in the ninth inning, a runner on base, and the Dodgers trailing by a run, Gibson, benched with a leg injury, pinch hit a game-winning homer off Oakland's relief ace, Dennis Eckersley. As Gibson limped around the bases, the Athletics seemed in shock. They never recovered and lost the Series in five games.

Walter O'Malley made thousands of enemies when he tore his team from Brooklyn in 1957. But his great experiment, making major league baseball a coast-to-coast game, has been an unqualified success, and his stadium in Chavez Ravine has been matched by few others.

Kirk Gibson was mobbed by his teammates after his dramatic ninth-inning home run in the opening game of the 1988 World Series between L.A. and the Athletics at Dodger Stadium. Above is a ticket for game two of the Series.

SHEA STADIUM
Queens, New York

1964–

The left and right field walls at Shea are 338 feet from the plate, the power alleys 371 feet, and dead center 410 feet. With the prevailing winds blowing in from behind center field, the park seems built for pitchers.

FOLLOWING THE DEPARTURE of the Dodgers and Giants after the 1957 season, New Yorkers demanded a National League franchise. They first tried to woo established teams to the city, and when that effort failed, seriously considered creating a third major circuit to be called the Continental League. The established major league team owners decided to expand for greater profits rather than fight, so New York and Houston were granted franchises for the 1962 season.

The New York nine, called the Mets (short for Metropolitans), played "camp ball"—it was so awful and so funny that boys attending summer camps could virtually have done as well. At first, during 1962 and 1963, the Mets played in the Polo Grounds but the old park, while fulfilling the Mets' desire to connect the new team with the old ones, was as inadequate for them as it had been for the Giants. Mayor Robert Wagner had promised, as a condition of the city's being granted the franchise, to build a new stadium, and work began on the facility in October 1961. Because Wagner's longtime friend and confidant, William A. Shea, had been the man most responsible for acquiring the franchise, the new stadium was named after him.

A legendary altercation took place at Shea during the third game of the 1973 National League Championship Series when the Reds' Pete Rose and the Mets' Buddy Harrelson (#3) slugged it out after Rose's hard slide into second base. When he returned to his position in left field, Rose was pelted with fruit by irate Met fans.

(Opposite) Jubilant New Yorkers swarmed all over the field after their lowly Mets took game five and the World Series from the heavily favored Baltimore Orioles on October 16, 1969.

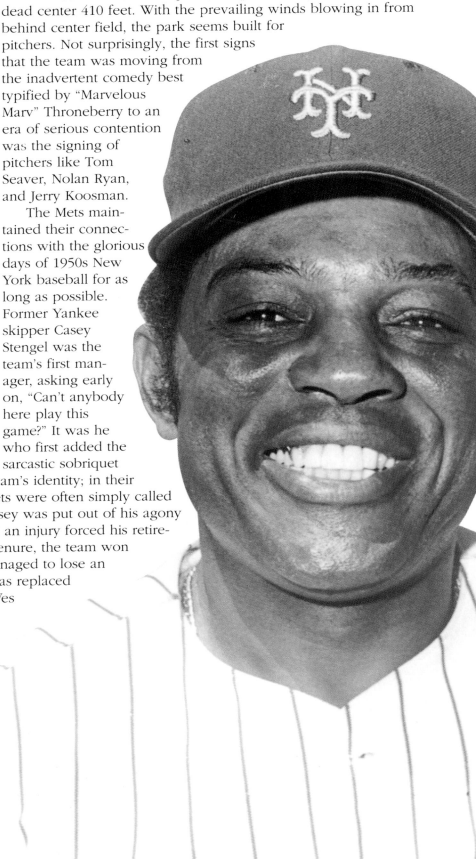

Shea Stadium is high. There are four levels of stands, with the upper grandstands almost as horizontally close to the action as the lower ones. As a result of this configuration, the steps are steep, and complaints of acrophobia are not uncommon. Grandstand seating is in the form of a broken circle with center field devoid of stands. There, 25 feet beyond the center field wall, an enormous scoreboard, 86 feet high and 175 feet long, visible from all angles of the stadium, dominates the scene. The left and right field walls are 338 feet from the plate, the power alleys 371 feet, and dead center 410 feet. With the prevailing winds blowing in from behind center field, the park seems built for pitchers. Not surprisingly, the first signs that the team was moving from the inadvertent comedy best typified by "Marvelous Marv" Throneberry to an era of serious contention was the signing of pitchers like Tom Seaver, Nolan Ryan, and Jerry Koosman.

The Mets maintained their connections with the glorious days of 1950s New York baseball for as long as possible. Former Yankee skipper Casey Stengel was the team's first manager, asking early on, "Can't anybody here play this game?" It was he who first added the sarcastic sobriquet "Amazin'" to the team's identity; in their worst days, the Mets were often simply called "the Amazin's." Casey was put out of his agony in mid-1965, when an injury forced his retirement. During his tenure, the team won 175 games and managed to lose an amazin' 404. He was replaced by an old Giant, Wes Westrum, under whose

Don Clendenon was one of the Mets' heroes during the miracle season of 1969. This ticket is for the third game of the 1969 World Series at Shea Stadium. It was a 5-0 victory for the Mets with homers by Eddie Kranepool and Tommie Agee.

Willie Mays ended his career where it started—in New York.

tutelage the Mets managed to lose 237 times in two-and-a-half years. Curiously, the more they lost, the more New York loved them. Attendance at Shea outstripped that at Yankee Stadium during a period of major Yankee success. A New Yorker drawing of the time depicted several dejected Mets walking into the dugout as someone consoled them by saying, "Cheer up. You can't lose them all."

But under Gil Hodges, late of the Dodgers, the team's fortunes turned around, and in 1969, they won the National League Eastern Division handily, then beat the Atlanta Braves 3-0 in the divisional playoffs (the first year of such contests) and (amazingly) defeated the powerful Baltimore Orioles 4-1 in the World Series, with three victories coming before the hometown fans. As they had all year, the wins came as a result of multiplayer heroics. Don Clendenon hit three homers in the Series, and Tommy Agee hit one homer and made two remarkable catches in game three, as did Ron Swoboda, always an adventure in right field. Unfortunately, the World Series victory was accompanied by fans tearing up the turf. This custom, once established, became a regular event whenever the Mets won a championship at home.

Neon art depicting ballplayers in various playing positions adorns Shea Stadium's exterior facade.

Other New York players from the 1950s were sent to the Mets for their last at bats. Duke Snider played for the team for a year in 1963, and ten years later, Willie Mays finished his career at Shea. Yogi Berra, the only man in America who could match the verbal shenanigans of his former chief, Casey Stengel, managed the team from 1972 until 1975, during which time—in 1973—the Mets won their second pennant, defeating a strong Cincinnati team led by Pete Rose. It was during the play-offs that Rose became involved in a legendary altercation at Shea. It came in the fifth inning of game three, after Rose had savagely slid into shortstop Bud Harrelson at second base, starting a bench-clearing fracas. When he returned to his position in left field, Rose was pelted with fruit by irate Met fans. Only the calming efforts of Berra, Mays, Seaver, and others prevented the home team

Seen above is Tom Seaver, the first of the Mets' super-star pitchers. In the miracle season of 1969, he posted a record of 25-7. Another of the heroes of 1969 was Jerry Koosman (above, right), who had a record of 17-9 and two World Series wins against the Orioles.

from losing by forfeit. After the victory over Cincinnati, the Mets were doomed to meet the powerful Oakland A's in the World Series. They played over their heads for a while—they were actually leading three games to two after winning two of three contests at Shea—but when they returned to Oakland, the A's regained their composure and swept the last two games, taking the second of their three consecutive Series victories.

For a long time, the most dramatic event in Shea was the great Seaver's eight-and-one-third innings of perfect ball against the Cubs in 1969. But this event was eclipsed during the sixth game of the 1986 World Series against the Boston Red Sox. When the Series began, it looked as though neither team wanted to win, each losing two games in their own park. But after the Sox took the fifth game at Fenway, they returned to Shea confident that their long World Series drought, which dated to the selling of Babe Ruth in 1919, was about to end. It seemed they were right; after nine-and-a-half innings in game six, the Sox led by two runs—and the first two Mets in the 10th were easily retired.

Television announcers were declaring that Bruce Hurst, a Boston pitcher, was the Series MVP; but on the field, Gary Carter and then Kevin Mitchell were busy hitting singles. With two strikes on him, Ray Knight blooped another single to center, enabling Carter to score and bringing Mitchell to third. Boston manager John McNamara brought in Bob Stanley, his closer, to face Mookie Wilson. With a 2-2 count (Wilson having fouled off four offerings), Stanley threw a wild pitch, allowing Mitchell to scamper home and tie the game, 5-5. After fouling off two more, Wilson sent an easy grounder toward first baseman Bill Buckner, but the ball bounded through Buck's gimpy legs and Knight raced

In the 10th inning of the sixth game of the 1986 World Series at Shea Stadium, the Red Sox' Bob Stanley threw this wild pitch to the Mets' Mookie Wilson, allowing the tying run to score from third. Moments later, Wilson hit a weak grounder between Bill Buckner's legs, and the Mets won one of the most exciting games in World Series history.

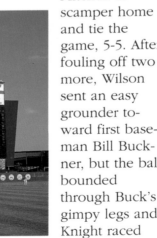

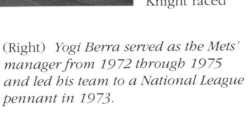

(Right) Shea Stadium's enormous scoreboard is set beyond the right center field wall. It is 86 feet high and 175 feet long and is visible from every angle of the stadium,

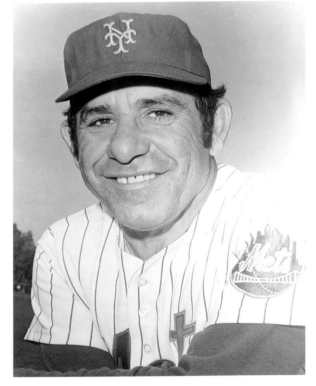

(Right) Yogi Berra served as the Mets' manager from 1972 through 1975 and led his team to a National League pennant in 1973.

Casey Stengel: The Mets' Field General

Casey Stengel's managerial career had three distinct phases. The first took place between 1934 and 1943, when he spent eight remarkably unsuccessful seasons managing the Brooklyn Dodgers and the Boston Braves. Phase two began in 1949, when the New York Yankees inexplicably named him their new skipper, although his teams had never finished better than fifth place. In a dozen Bronx seasons, Casey's teams won 10 American League pennants and nine World Championships, a record that placed him among the best managers in baseball history.

Why Stengel began phase three is anybody's guess. But at age 71, he accepted an offer to manage the Mets in their first season. His new team was awful. A terrible mix of veteran castoffs and unproven youngsters, Casey's New Yorkers invented new ways to lose baseball games. They dropped foul pop-ups, heaved balls into the upper decks, and missed bags as

they rounded the bases. But Casey, a man who had seen baseball's best and worst, took the ineptitude in stride, verbally exhibiting a wit and wisdom that endeared him to baseball fans around the country.

"Don't cut my throat," he once told his barber after a tough loss. "I'm saving that for myself." When someone asked him about the Mets' dismal 40-120 record during their maiden season, Casey quipped, "I wonder how we ever won forty. That damn team showed me ways to lose I never knew existed."

Though Stengel frequently played the buffoon in public, especially during his seasons with the Mets, heady players like Warren Spahn, Tony Kubek, and Billy Martin claimed that he was a genius on the field. But to Casey, managing was easy. "What the hell is it but telling the umpire who's gonna play and then watching them play," he once said. "The best thing to do is to have players who can hit right-handed and left-handed and hit farther one way and farther sometimes the other way and run like the wind."

home with the winning run. The curse of the Bambino had struck again. The next game was a foregone conclusion. All the world knew that the Sox would lose, and they did, again as a result of late-inning Shea Stadium rallies.

For the present generation of Met fans, the events of 1986 were truly amazing. Older New Yorkers were only partly satisfied—if only they had happened at Ebbets Field!

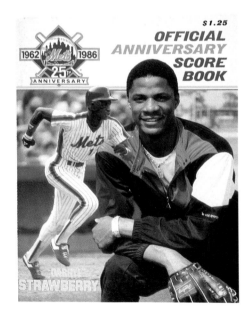

This scorecard, from the championship season of 1986, celebrates Shea's 25th anniversary. It features Darryl Strawberry, one of that season's many heroes.

This photo shows how to build a domed stadium—Texas style.

The dimensions of the Astrodome's playing field have fluctuated over the years. The power alleys, for example, were 375 feet in 1965, 390 in 1966, 378 in 1972, back to 390 in 1977, and then 370 in 1985. Center field has rocked back and forth between 400 and 406 feet.

ASTRODOME
Houston, Texas

1965–

Judge Roy Hofheinz, a Texas political figure, played a large role in bringing the Astrodome to completion.

IN WHAT PASSES FOR SUBTLETY IN TEXAS, the promoters of the first domed stadium modestly dubbed their creation "the Eighth Wonder of the World." Putting it another way, in Houston did Hofheinz a stately pleasure-dome decree.

Judge Roy Hofheinz was the Texas politico who, with lots of other people's money, built the Astrodome to replace the temporary grounds constructed for the new Houston franchise in 1962. That original monstrosity, called Colt Stadium, opened for play even before the concrete had fully set. It was designed as a quick fix until the team's true home could be completed, but for the two years that it was in use, it was a plague on the teams that played in it and spectators as well. There were many problems with Colt Stadium, but the biggest was the mosquito infestation. Indeed, the Astros' home was the only major league ballpark of this century that had to be sprayed regularly between innings to kill mosquitoes, a fruitless task because they always came back with a vengeance. Sandy Koufax once complained that the bugs flying around his head and attacking him were twin-engine jobs.

The site of the old mosquito-infested field is now part

In the stadium's early days, fielders complained about the difficulty of seeing high fly balls due to reflections from the dome's translucent plastic panels. In this 1965 photo, Houston infielder Bob Lillis compares two pair of sunglasses to see which will more effectively combat the glare.

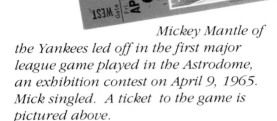

Mickey Mantle of the Yankees led off in the first major league game played in the Astrodome, an exhibition contest on April 9, 1965. Mick singled. A ticket to the game is pictured above.

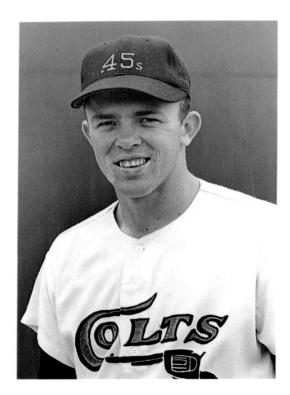

The Astros' disastrous early years resulted, in part, from the team's uncanny ability to trade away superstars just before they reached their peaks. Among them was Jerry Grote, pictured here, who went on to play a key role with the championship Mets of 1969.

of the enormous, 30,000-car parking lot that surrounds the Astrodome. The Dome, which opened in 1965 (when the Colts became the Astros), hosts both baseball and football. In its early years, it also housed the Countdown Cafeteria, the Trailblazer Restaurant, a VIP suite with an imitation medieval chapel, and an imitation sidewalk cafe, but some of these accommodations have since been removed. Today, skyboxes, which in 1977 cost a modest $15,000 per annum, adjoin club rooms and, according to Roger Kahn's A Season in the Sun, are equipped with "telephones, radios, bars and furniture ranging from French Provincial to Texas Gauche." Near the Dome, Hofheinz built four hotels, a convention center (Astrohall), and an amusement park (Astroworld).

Given Houston's heat, humidity, frequent rain, and mosquito population, baseball purists can forgive the city its dome. The stadium's other contribution to the National Pastime—Astroturf—is, of course, unforgivable. Ironically, the abomination, euphemistically called "artificial surface," was not in the original design at all. It was imposed on the Dome's management by the vicissitudes of nature. A special kind of Bermuda grass for indoor use, known as Tifway 419, was originally installed and worked fine until fielders started to complain that reflections from the dome's translu-

cent plastic panels prevented them from seeing high fly balls. To solve this problem, the dome was painted, but that prevented natural light from entering the park, and the grass died. Something had to be done, and the Monsanto Company, as the story goes, came to the rescue, offering to carpet the field for $375,000. Hofheinz countered by threatening to charge Monsanto $375,000 for the right to install it and call it "Astroturf." A compromise was reached, and the playing fields of America have never been the same.

Some statistics will give mathematical shape to the enclosure, which—whether one hates it or loves it—must be seen as one of the engineering marvels of our age. Exactly 4,796 panes of plastic comprise the dome, in the center of which, 208 feet above second base, is a gondola that keeps a television camera afloat. The stands hold 45,011 spectators for baseball. The dimensions of the playing field have varied according to whether a temporary wall in the outfield was installed or not. Management cannot seem to make up its mind about that barrier. The foul poles in 1965 were 340 feet from home plate, 330 feet in 1972, back to 340 in 1977, and re-shrunk to 330 in 1985. Power alleys have suffered the same kind of fluctuations: 375 feet in 1965, 390 in 1966, 378 in 1972, back to 390 in 1977, and then 370 in 1985. Center field has rocked back and forth between 400 and 406 feet.

Regardless of the changes in the dimensions of the field, the Astrodome has always been a pitcher's park. The ball simply does not carry here. The players claim that Astrodome air is dead, and the paucity of Astro home run hitters justifies that opinion. No Astro has won a league home run title, though Glenn Davis finished second in 1986 and 1988 with modest totals of 31 and 30 respectively. The team recognized early on that the long ball would not be a factor in the Dome and tried to win with speedsters like Joe Morgan and Sonny Jackson, both of whom took treacherous leads off of first base while the animated scoreboard flashed images of go-go dancers urging them to swipe second base. Not surprisingly,

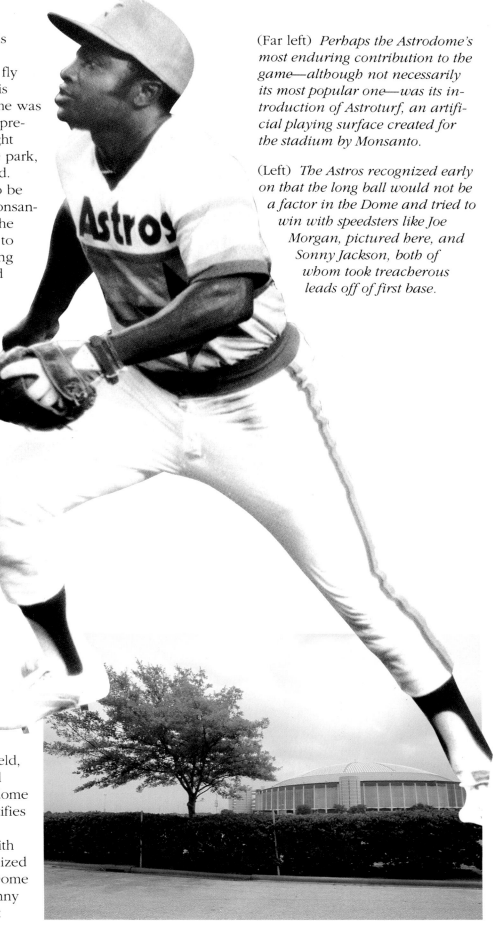

(Far left) *Perhaps the Astrodome's most enduring contribution to the game—although not necessarily its most popular one—was its introduction of Astroturf, an artificial playing surface created for the stadium by Monsanto.*

(Left) *The Astros recognized early on that the long ball would not be a factor in the Dome and tried to win with speedsters like Joe Morgan, pictured here, and Sonny Jackson, both of whom took treacherous leads off of first base.*

From afar, the Astrodome looks more like a convention center than a ballpark.

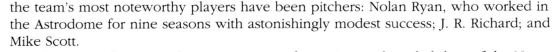

the team's most noteworthy players have been pitchers: Nolan Ryan, who worked in the Astrodome for nine seasons with astonishingly modest success; J. R. Richard; and Mike Scott.

The Astros' first several seasons were as frustrating as the salad days of the New York Mets, their partners in expansion. In 1962, they finished eighth, from 1963 to 1965 ninth, in 1966 eighth again, and in 1967 ninth. The following year, they landed in the cellar, and they closed the decade with a fifth-place finish in the newly created six-team Western Division. In the 1970s, they achieved second place twice in an otherwise dreary decade of futility; reports hinted that the team would go bankrupt.

These disastrous results were caused, in part, by the team's uncanny ability to trade away superstars just before they reached their peaks. For example, in the Astros' early years, they let go of Rusty Staub and Jerry Grote, later spark-plugs of the championship Mets; Joe Morgan, a two-time MVP with the Reds; Dave Guisti, a capable starting pitcher for the Pirates; and Mike Cuellar, a Cy Young Award-winner with Baltimore.

In the late 1970s, new management brought better player retention, and the Astros began to shine like the heavens for which they were named. In 1980, they won the National League's Western Division title but lost the league championship to Philadelphia in a memorable five-game Series. In the fifth and deciding game, the Phillies rallied for five runs in the eighth inning to take a 7-5 lead, but the Astros came back to tie and force the game into the fourth straight overtime contest of the Series. Houston lost it in the 10th inning. The next few years saw the Astros bouncing around the middle of the Western Division rankings, but in 1986 they copped the crown again, this time having to face the favored Mets in the playoffs. In the Series' sixth and final game, at the

Nolan Ryan was 106-94 as an Astro from 1980 through 1988. He threw one of his career no-hitters while wearing Houston's uniform. Ryan graced the cover of the Astros program above, which commemorated the Dome's 20th anniversary.

Dome, the Astros went ahead 3-0 in the first inning but lost the lead in the ninth. The next three frames were scoreless; then each team put a run on the board in the 14th inning. In the 16th, the Mets scored three runs, and the Astros answered with

two. They had lost again but had experienced the glory of playing in

 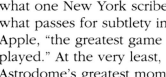

what one New York scribe called, in what passes for subtlety in the Big Apple, "the greatest game ever played." At the very least, it was the Astrodome's greatest moment.

(Above) *The Astrodome's sky boxes provide great views of the game.*

The 1986 National League Championship Series: Game Six

In 1986, the New York Mets reached the World Series by winning the sixth game of the National League Championship Series with a score of 7-6. But this simple statement does not begin to describe the drama of that final game in the Astrodome.

At first the game looked like an easy victory for the home team in a contest that both sides thought they had to win—Houston to stay alive for a seventh game, New York to avoid facing Mike Scott, the Astros' ace, if that seventh game were necessary. In the first inning, the Astros scored three times and sent the Mets' starter, Bob Ojeda, to the showers. After that, however, the home-towners were stopped for the next 12 innings.

But the Mets could not get their offense going either, managing only two hits and a walk until the top of the ninth inning. Then, with the specter of Scott looming ominously before them, the Mets rallied, getting a triple from pinch hitter Lenny Dykstra, a single from Mookie Wilson, a double from Keith Hernandez, two walks, and a sacrifice fly from Ray Knight. Three runs had scored, and the game was knotted, 3-3.

That was the end of the scoring until the 14th inning, when the Mets' Wally Backman singled home Daryl Strawberry. But in the Astros' half of the frame, with two outs, Billy Hatcher hit the only homer of the game and again tied the score.

The 15th inning was scoreless, but in the 16th, the Mets rallied again. Two hits, two walks, and two wild pitches brought New York three runs—surely a safe lead, they thought. But in their half, Houston struck back. A walk and three singles plated two runs.

Two runners were on base, two men were out, and the Mets' weary reliever, Jesse Orosco, was pitching against Kevin Bass, the Astros' leading hitter. Bass worked the count full; then Orosco threw a sharp breaking ball past him, and the first-ever League Championship Series between two expansion teams was over. So was the longest post-season game in the history of baseball.

Jesse Orosco of the Mets leaps for the sky after striking out Kevin Bass for the final out in the pennant-clinching 7-6 victory in 16 innings on October 15, 1986.

The paucity of Astro home run hitters supports the notion that the baseball simply does not carry well in the Astrodome. Although no Astro has ever won the home run title, Glenn Davis, pictured here, finished second in 1986 with 31 and in 1988 with 30.

This program is a souvenir from the 1980 season, the first in which the Astros won a division title.

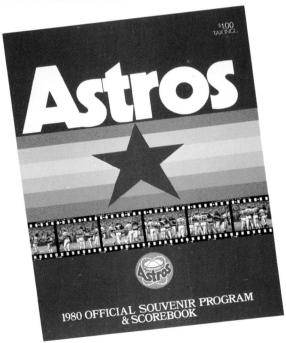

Astros

$1.00 TAX INCL.

1980 OFFICIAL SOUVENIR PROGRAM & SCOREBOOK

BUSCH MEMORIAL STADIUM
St. Louis, Missouri

1966-

Before the seventh game of the 1982 World Series, Augie Busch rides into his stadium on the Budweiser beer wagon pulled by the famous Clydesdales.

BUSCH MEMORIAL STADIUM is deceiving. It looks as if it should be surrounded by acres of suburban parking lots where interstates intersect. The stadium is perfectly round, spacious in seating capacity (50,000 plus), with a symmetrical field—330 feet in left and right fields, 386 feet in the power alleys, and 414 feet in center—and walls that are uniform in height at 102 feet. But Busch Stadium, the prototype for the superstructures built to replace the crumbling pre-World War I parks in the old National League cities (it relieved Sportsman's Park), is right, smack-dab in the middle of downtown St. Louis. It has parking space for more than 17,000 cars—but in a series of multi-story garages and small lots. It is accessible by public transportation, so when suburbanites from University City or Ladue want to see a game, they just come to town—and they do so in large numbers.

Completed in 1966, Busch Stadium was part of a massive urban renewal project, one of two St. Louis was mounting simultaneously in the mid-1960s (the other was in the area around St. Louis University). Both were highly successful endeavors, though the downtown project with its new Gateway Arch and stadium was glitzier than the

A statue of demigod Stan Musial greets visitors outside Busch Stadium, though "Stan the Man" never played here.

(Opposite) The patented Ozzie Smith backflip has long been a Busch Stadium crowd pleaser.

Southpaw John Tudor, who had trouble pitching in Fenway Park when he was with the Red Sox, found success as a Cardinal in Busch Stadium.

renovation near Philharmonic Hall, created out of a converted motion-picture palace. Still, Mayor Alfonso Cervantes was no impossible dreamer when he set the projects in motion.

The ballpark is a tribute to the city, the team, and the beer mogul for whom it is named. At other stadiums, the seventh-inning stretch is accompanied by "Take Me Out to the Ball Game." At the home of the Cardinals, it is the familiar TV jingle for Budweiser beer. The scoreboard also has pictures of Clydesdales pulling along a suds truck. (The actual horses pull the real wagon around on opening day.) The scoreboard is one of the marvels of the game's modern era.

In addition to incidentals such as the local and out-of-town scores, it also shows re-plays (even contro-versial ones), person-al inter-views, and high-lights of the last game. Strangely enough, how-ever, it is awk-wardly placed so that people sit-ting in the outfield seats cannot see the show.

Architecturally, the most interesting part of the stadium is the rim along the top tier, a series of connected arches angling inward—a tribute to the city's foremost monument and to its historic role as the Gate-way to the West.

The title was well deserved in the mid-19th century but ignored by the baseball powers who placed the St. Louis Cards in the National League's Eastern Division

Perhaps the greatest Busch Stadium Cardinal was Lou Brock, who could hit the ball to the gaps, stretch the singles into doubles, and steal a base. He is shown here on the day he celebrated his retirement, September 9, 1979.

(and Atlanta in the West). Outside the park, visitors are greeted by the statue of a man who never played there but who is a local demigod. Stan "the Man" Musial still crouches, bat in hand, eye on the ball, ready to whack one for the distance.

Originally the grass was real, though for some reason never very good. It always looked blotchy. Rather than fix the problem, management decided to go modern and defoliate with artificial turf in 1970. The dirt infield was kept for another few years, until the opening of the 1974 season when, except for the sliding pits around the bases, the entire field was covered with Astroturf. Playing on Astroturf has been compared to shooting pool with a superball, and, in fact, the vast distances to the fences and the speed of the artificial surface have combined to make Busch Sta-

This panoramic view of Busch Stadium shows many of the park's 53,000 cardinal-red seats.

The Speedy Mr. McGee

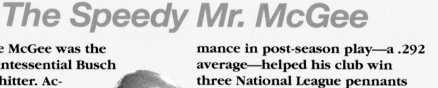

Willie McGee was the quintessential Busch Stadium hitter. Acquired by the Cardinals after the 1981 season in a trade with the Yankees, McGee played nine seasons in St. Louis, eight of which were very productive. He lacked power, never hitting more than 11 homers in a season, but earned his salary slapping line drives to the far reaches of Busch's broad artificial lawns and legging out extra base hits. He won National League batting titles in 1985 and 1990, the latter honor earned despite a late-season trade to the Oakland A's. His achievements during the 1985 campaign—a .353 average, 216 hits, 18 triples, 114 runs scored, 56 stolen bases—earned him the Most Valuable Player Award.

Tall and slender, McGee patrolled Busch Stadium's center field with grace and style, winning four Gold Glove Awards for fielding excellence. With McGee in center, the Cards won three Eastern Division titles. His solid perfor-

mance in post-season play—a .292 average—helped his club win three National League pennants and the 1982 World Series.

Two time National batting champ Willie McGee, shown here homering in game four of the 1985 World Series, was the quintessential Busch Stadium hitter.

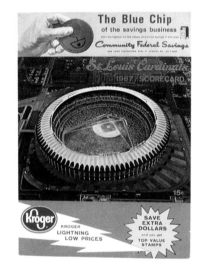

This scorecard is from 1967, the year the Cardinals beat the Boston Red Sox in the World Series.

The jersey collection at Busch Stadium illustrates how the Cardinals' uniform has changed over the years.

dium one of pro baseball's premier parks for pitchers and singles hitters. The legendary greats of St. Louis—the Dean brothers, the Gashouse Gang, Stan the Man— never played in Busch, but pitchers such as Bob Gibson, who won 251 games and earned a spot in Cooperstown, and John Tutor have excelled there, while hitters of the Lou Brock, Curt Flood, Willie McGee, and Ozzie Smith mode have made their presence felt by virtue of their speed, both on the basepaths and at their defensive positions.

Whether the system of relying on great pitchers and fast batsmen has worked is questionable. Since Busch Stadium opened in 1966, the Cards have won five National League pennants—two in the 1960s and three in the 1980s—and the World Series in 1967 and 1982. What happened during the 1970s? Except for 1973, when no one seemed to want the flag and the Mets took it with a meager .509 winning percentage, the Phillies and Pirates copped every National League Eastern Division championship. Those teams relied on power—remember Pittsburgh's "Lumber Company"?

Whitey Herzog's teams were Busch's best, winning pennants in 1982, 1985, and 1987. Those squads—featuring McGee, Ozzie, and (in 1985 and 1987) the speedy Vince Coleman—hit few homers but stroked the ball into the alleys and circled the bases quickly. The 1982 team beat the slugging, slow-footed Milwaukee Brewers—"the Brew Crew"—in the World Series, despite hitting only four round-trippers. But even Whitey's good teams were sometimes lost when their singles hitters went on the road and played in parks more suited to the long ball. A case in point was the 1987 Series against the Twins. The Cards won all three games at Busch Stadium but dropped all four in Minnesota's "Homer Dome." Cardinal batters could only manage two home runs off of Minnesota's moundsmen.

Whitey Herzog's teams were Busch Stadium's best. At right "the White Rat" is shown handing the ball to his top reliever, Bruce Sutter, in game two of the 1982 World Series. A ticket to the game is pictured above along with a souvenir from the "Suds Series," which pitted the Cards against the Milwaukee Brewers.

Vince Coleman was another Busch Stadium speedster. He is shown here running by the outstretched glove of Terry Francona as he beats out a bunt.

Sometimes the Cards have been hoist by their own petard with their emphasis on slickness, but the St. Louis rooters do not seem to mind. They dress in red and flock downtown to sit in their red seats—all seats at Busch are cardinal colored—and they cheer loudly and enthusiastically as Ozzie flips backward to his position. They know that someday another championship series will be played under the arches.

The arches running along the top of Busch Stadium complement the famous Gateway Arch shown in the background.

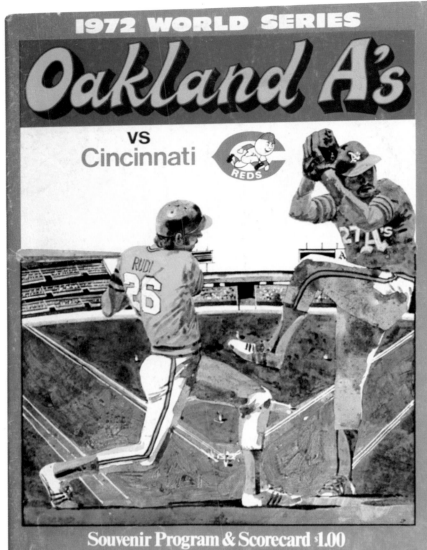

1972 WORLD SERIES

Oakland A's

VS
Cincinnati

RUDI
26

27 A's

Souvenir Program & Scorecard $1.00

(Left) *The cover of this 1972 World Series program features two of Charles Finley's key players: Joe Rudi and Jim "Catfish" Hunter.*

A field box–seat ticket for game two of the 1989 World Series.

(Right) *Shortstop Bert Campaneris signs autographs before the fifth game of the 1972 World Series, the first Fall Classic played at the Oakland Coliseum.*

OAKLAND-ALAMEDA
COUNTY COLISEUM
Oakland, California

`1968–`

As this shot of the Oakland Coliseum's box office suggests, much of the stadium is below ground level.

7HE ATHLETICS closely followed the advice of the mid-19th-century New York Tribune editor, Horace Greeley, whose famous words—"Go west, young man"—inspired thousands of easterners to pack their belongings and seek their fortunes in the lands past the Mississippi River. After spending their first 55 seasons in Philadelphia, the A's journeyed to Kansas City, Missouri, in 1955 and remained there for 13 pennantless seasons. Then after the 1967 season, they moved even further west, settling in across the bay from Horace Stoneham's San Francisco Giants.

The A's owner, Chicago insurance man Charles Finley, moved his club to a place rich in baseball tradition. The San Francisco Bay area had produced Tony Lazzeri, the DiMaggio brothers, Billy Martin, and a host of other major league notables. For decades, before the Giants and A's had arrived, the San Francisco Seals and the Oakland Oaks of the Pacific Coast League had drawn well and had supplied the major leagues with a steady stream of talented players. Even Casey Stengel had once managed the Oaks to a pennant. From 1913 through 1957, the Oaks had played at Oakland Ballpark (located in neighboring

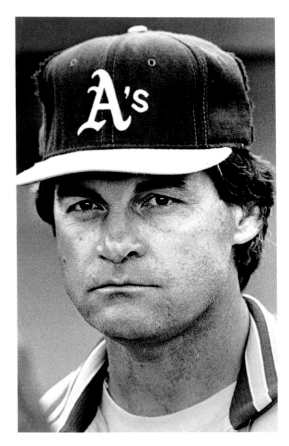

The Oakland Coliseum's current manager-in-residence, Tony LaRussa, is considered to be the game's most brilliant strategist by many.

This 1973 World Series ticket features a kicking mule, the A's mascot during the years that Charles Finley owned the team.

Reggie Jackson shows the powerful swing that resulted in 563 lifetime homers. While playing in Oakland, he won two American League home run titles.

(Right) The Coliseum's old scoreboard keeps fans abreast of happenings around the major league.

Emoryville), a ramshackle, 12,000-seat arena with all the charm of Ebbets Field. Given the area's long-standing association with baseball, Finley figured that his A's could enjoy the kind of success that had eluded them in Kansas City.

When Finley's A's arrived in Oakland for the 1968 season, the Oakland-Alameda County Coliseum was waiting to receive them. It had been built with taxpayers' money two years earlier for the American Football League's Oakland Raiders, the bruising gridiron squad that has since deserted the Bay area for Los Angeles. Like many of the superstructures that were built in the 1960s to accommodate both football and baseball, the Oakland Coliseum is circular in shape and symmetrical in design. Set deep in the ground on a tract of land alongside the C.W. Nimitz Freeway, the stadium is barely visible from afar. As fans approach the park, they descend an ivy-covered slope to the ticket windows.

Architecturally, the stadium is unspectacular. To older fans, it lacks the intimacy and charm of the classic urban ballparks, and to contemporary fans, it fails to provide the engineering theatrics of the domed stadiums. Three decks of uncovered grandstand seats surround the playing field, and a single tier of bleacher seats is set behind 10-foot-high outfield walls. In total, it accommodates about 48,600 customers.

The dimensions of the grass playing field typify those of the stadiums built in the 1960s: from home plate, it is 330 feet to the foul poles, 375 feet to the power alleys, and about 400 feet to dead center field. Affecting play significantly are the wide tracts of foul territory between the foul lines and the grandstands. Oakland hitters maintain that these huge areas cost them 10 points each on their yearly batting averages. Foul pop-ups that would drift 10 rows back into the stands at Fenway Park and give the batter another swing can easily be captured by an infielder in the Oakland Coliseum. Indeed, no Oakland hitter has ever won a batting title, though Carney Lansford finished second by only three points in 1989.

Oakland's stadium may be drab, but its team has often been spectacular. The A's

Charles O. Finley: The A's Unorthodox Owner

Charles Oscar Finley had humble beginnings. The son of a steel-worker, he followed his father into the Gary, Indiana, mills right after his high school graduation. But he peddled insurance policies at night, and in a few years, his shrewd salesmanship had allowed him to quit the mills and establish his own insurance company. By his mid-thirties, Finley was a millionaire. In 1960, he realized a lifelong dream—to own a major league baseball team—when he acquired the controlling interest in the lowly Kansas City Athletics.

Unlike the other baseball owners of his day, Finley took an active role in his team's on-the-field activities. He engineered trades, badgered groundskeepers, and even telephoned the dugout during games to make suggestions to his manager. He also introduced promotional gimmicks, such as postgame fireworks, a team mule, and outlandish yellow and green uniforms—all of which were considered bush league by his fellow owners.

But over time, Finley built a winning team. His young players—Reggie Jackson, Catfish Hunter, and Rollie Fingers—reached their primes just after the club moved to Oakland, where they won three straight World Series. But success did not endear Finley to his manager or his players, who resented his constant interference in their affairs. In the 1973 World Series, for example, when Finley forced second baseman Mike Andrews to leave the club with a trumped-up injury after Andrews' two errors had cost the A's a game, Hunter, Jackson, and others rallied around their teammate, and he returned to the lineup the next day.

In 1980, Finley sold the A's after they had slipped from contention. But his style of team ownership lived on in another autocratic baseball proprietor—George Steinbrenner, the former majority shareholder of the New York Yankees.

Charles Finley justifiably flashes the victory sign; during his tenure as owner, the Athletics won three straight World Series championships.

This shot of the Oakland Coliseum's playing field clearly shows the wide section of foul territory along each baseline—a friend to the pitchers, an enemy to the hitters.

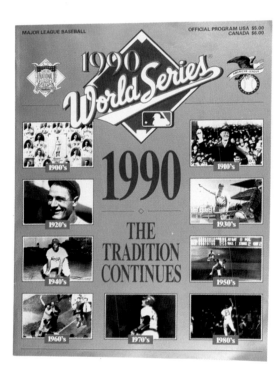

finished in last place the year before moving to Oakland, but their roster featured colorful and talented young players such as Jim "Catfish" Hunter, Reggie Jackson, Bert Campaneris, and John "Blue Moon" Odom—the foundation of the squad that would dominate baseball in the early 1970s. In 1968, their first Oakland season, the A's nudged their record above .500. During the next few years, the team added stars like Sal Bando, Joe Rudi, Rollie Fingers, and Vida Blue. In 1971, Finley's club won 101 games and captured the American League's Western Division title. Oakland was vanquished in three games by the Orioles in the playoffs, but in 1972, the A's were back in post-season play, and this time they eliminated Detroit in the American League Championship Series and then upset the powerful Cincinnati Reds in a tightly played World Series, during which six of the seven games were decided by a single run.

The 1972 A's were only the first of Finley's champions. Oakland returned to the World Series the next two seasons, besting the Mets in 1973 and the Dodgers the following October. They won with strong pitching, clutch hitting, and a pizzazz matched by few teams over the past two decades. Finley fired managers and badgered his players, and the A's fought among themselves in the locker room— all of which produced a reckless, swashbuckling attitude that translated into victories on the playing field.

But after those championship seasons, free agency broke up Finley's club, as Hunter, Jackson, Rudi, Fingers, and others played out their contracts and joined other teams or were traded away before they could exercise their options. By 1977, the A's had played their way into the cellar, and the fans had stopped coming. The team endured some

The concession stands at the Coliseum are empty now, but they will be busy enough selling hot dogs and beer when the big crowd arrives.

This 1990 World Series program commemorates great moments in the history of the Fall Classic.

Left hander Vida Blue played a key role on the teams that hung three straight world championship banners at the Oakland Coliseum.

miserable seasons, and its stadium became known as the "Oakland Mausoleum." Attendance plummeted to under 400,000. Billy Martin came aboard as manager in 1980 and pushed the team to respectability, but the A's were on the skids again two years later. Finley had sold out by then, and the team's new owners, members of the Haas family, tried patiently to rebuild the depleted franchise.

Like most contemporary stadiums, the Oakland Coliseum has swanky suites for corporate customers.

The turnaround began in mid-1986, when Tony LaRussa was hired to manage the team. He made Dave Stewart a starting pitcher and patiently tutored his talented youngsters, Mark McGwire and Jose Canseco. In 1987, the team finished at .500. The next year, Canseco blossomed into a superstar, Dennis Eckersley developed into the league's best relief pitcher, and the A's won 104 games and the American League pennant. An upset victory by the Dodgers denied Oakland a World Championship, but the following season, in the World Series interrupted by an earthquake, the A's beat their cross-bay rivals, the Giants, in four games. It was a most satisfying season for Bay-area fans, and 4.7 million of them patronized the Oakland Coliseum and Candlestick Park that summer.

The A's copped another American League flag in 1990, though they were surprised by the upstart Reds in the Fall Classic. Nonetheless, Jose Canseco, Rickey Henderson, Dennis Eckersley, and a score of other talented players are likely to keep Oakland Coliseum fans happy for several seasons to come.

A starting pitcher for much of his career, Dennis Eckersley came to Oakland and became the game's best relief man.

Manager Dick Howser led the Royals to the 1985 world championship. His tragic death from a brain tumor in 1987 was a great loss to the sport.

Between innings, Royals Stadium's 322-foot-wide fountain-and-waterfall complex entertains fans with a spectacular water show.

 R O Y A L S STADIUM

Kansas City, Missouri

1973–

Royals Stadium, set along Interstates 70 and 435, has been the home of the Kansas City Royals since 1973.

I **N 1969,** their first year in the American League, the Kansas City Royals played in old Municipal Stadium. Built in 1923, it was the former home of the Kansas City Monarchs of the Negro American League and the Kansas City Blues, a long-time Yankee farm team. The park had been expanded in 1955 to accommodate the Athletics, who stopped in Kansas City for 13 seasons on their westward trek from Philadelphia to Oakland, so it was large enough to house the Royals. But Jackson County officials believed that their new baseball franchise deserved a modern facility, one of which their fans could be proud. They began planning the Harry S. Truman Sports Complex, which would not only include a stadium for the Royals, but also a new home for the American Football Conference's Kansas City Chiefs.

The baseball park that opened in 1973 had much in common with the stadiums that had been erected during the late 1960s in Philadelphia and Pittsburgh. Like those superstructures, Royals Stadium was built outside the inner city and along major freeways, in this case interstates 70 and 435, and was surrounded by parking lots rather than a neighborhood. Like those contemporary National League

Royals Stadium requires the services of swift players like Frank White, pictured here. White was Kansas City's second baseman from 1973 through 1989.

fields, the playing surface at Royals Stadium was Astroturf, and the stadium itself, as well as the playing field, was symmetrical, a feature that distinguished many of the newer playing facilities.

But the Royals new home differed from the likes of Veterans Stadium in Philadelphia and Three Rivers in Pittsburgh in several important ways. First, because Royals Stadium would be used for baseball only, architect Joseph Spear designed a park that was modest in size, at least by 1970 standards. It seated a little more than 40,000 people—about the same capacity as old Ebbets Field. And the playing field, like those in older parks, was not totally enclosed by the grandstand. No seats in Royals Stadium are located beyond the outfield fences; instead a 322-foot-wide fountain-and-waterfall complex is set behind the outfield wall, offering patrons a spectacular water show between innings. A large crown with the Royals insignia is set atop the fountains.

In this photo, Pete LaCock is stealing second base in the first game of the 1978 American League Championship Series at Royals Stadium, but the home team lost the game by a score of 7-1 and the series, three games to one.

Spear designed the grandstand so that every fan would have an excellent view of the action on the diamond. The seats are arranged in two decks, and the grandstands are built close to the field, like those in the old parks. Each seat is aimed directly at second base.

The style of play that has evolved in Royals Stadium, however, is similar to the brand of baseball played in the Astroturfed fields in the National League. The distant outfield fences—330 feet down the foul lines, 385 feet in the power alleys, and 410 feet to straightaway center field— discourage the home run. And the slick, artificial playing surface favors batters who can slash the ball into the gaps between the outfielders and circle the bases quickly.

When Whitey Herzog took over the team as manager halfway through the 1975 season, he manned his club with swift-running, line-drive hitters, the same type of players that he would later employ when he managed the St. Louis Cardinals. His third baseman was the great George Brett, and his designated hitter was Hal McRae; both hit the ball in the alleys and ran the bases well. Amos Otis, Al Cowens, and Frank White were players from the same mold. With this talented cast, Herzog's Royals won American League Western Division titles in 1976, 1977, and 1978.

Whitey's problem, however, was that his Royals could not beat the fine New York

Yankee teams of the late 1970s. Each time they captured the division title, they lost in the American League Championship Series to the Yanks and were thus denied the opportunity to play in the World Series. The defeat in 1977 was particularly stinging. The Royals had won two of the first three games in the playoffs and needed to win only one more of the remaining two contests at Royals Stadium to advance to the World Series. The Yanks won game four, 6-4, but the Royals had a 3-2 lead entering the ninth inning of the deciding game. In the ninth, however, the Yankees rallied for three runs, ending the Royals' World Series hopes.

The Royals got revenge in 1980, however. A new manager, Jim Frey, was in charge, but the team's key players—Brett, McRae, Otis, and White—were still with the club, and a speedy newcomer, Willie Wilson,

Royals Stadium is decked out for its first World Series, the 1980 matchup between the Royals and the Philadelphia Phillies. A scorecard for the Series and a ticket for game one are at right.

was driving American League managers crazy with his crisp hitting and frequent base stealing. In that year's American League Championship Series, the Royals beat the Yanks three straight times, earning the right to face the Philadelphia Phillies in the World Series. Again, however, Royals fans were disappointed as the Phillies won the Series in six games.

Five years later, the Royals finally brought their fans a title. The team sputtered during the first half of the season, but manager Dick Howser rallied his troops and led them to the division title in a close pennant race. The Royals trailed the Toronto Blue Jays two games to none and then three to one in the Championship Series but came back to win it in seven games. In game four at Royals Stadium, George Brett had the finest day of his outstanding career. In a contest that the hometowners had to win, Brett got four hits, including two homers, scored four times, and drove in home three runs in the 6-5 Royal victory.

In the 1985 all-Missouri World Series, the Royals again came back after trailing two games to none and then three games to one. In game six, a tight pitching duel between the Cardinals' Danny Cox and the Royals' Charlie Leibrandt, the Royals trailed 1-0 going into the ninth inning. Only three outs from another World Series defeat, Kansas City, helped by an umpire's questionable call at first base, scored twice and lived to play another day. In game seven, the Royals beat the Cards 11-0, giving Kansas City its first World Series title.

In the late 1980s, Kansas City fell from contention as the powerful Oakland Athletics dominated the American League's Western Division. Nonetheless, the Royals have continued to draw fans to their clean, well-designed stadium set in a city rich in baseball history.

The speedy Willie Wilson patrolled the outfield and stole bases at Royals Stadium from 1976 through 1989.

(Above right) *George Brett, a three-time American League batting champ, is the quintessential Royals Stadium batter: a line-drive hitter whose hard smashes often find the gaps between the outfielders.*

The White Rat: Whitey Herzog

Whitey Herzog, one of contemporary baseball's most successful managers, had a mediocre playing career. He spent most of his eight big league seasons as a platoon player and bench warmer and retired with a .257 career batting average.

But perhaps thousands of innings on the bench had allowed Herzog to study the game in a way that the starting nine could not. After his retirement as a player in 1963, he had no trouble finding work in baseball as a scout and coach. In 1973, he was was hired to manage the Texas Rangers, but his club was awful, and he was fired before the season ended. He got a second chance two years later, when he was hired at mid-season to pilot a lackluster Kansas City Royals team. Under Herzog, the club straightened out, winning 41 of its last 66 games. The next season, Herzog's Royals won their first of three consecutive American League Western Division titles.

Herzog developed a reputation for building a solid pitching staff where none had previously existed, for using every man on his roster where he could be most effective, and for accommodating his team to his stadium. One of the first decisions he made in Kansas City was to replace two aging former stars, Vada Pinson and Cookie Rojas, with Al Cowens and Frank White, two youngsters who could use their speed to cover the slick Astroturf field at Royals Stadium.

The Royals fired Herzog after the 1979 season, but he was immediately hired by the St. Louis Cardinals. In his 11 seasons with the Redbirds, he brought Cardinal fans three National League pennants and, in 1982, a World Championship.

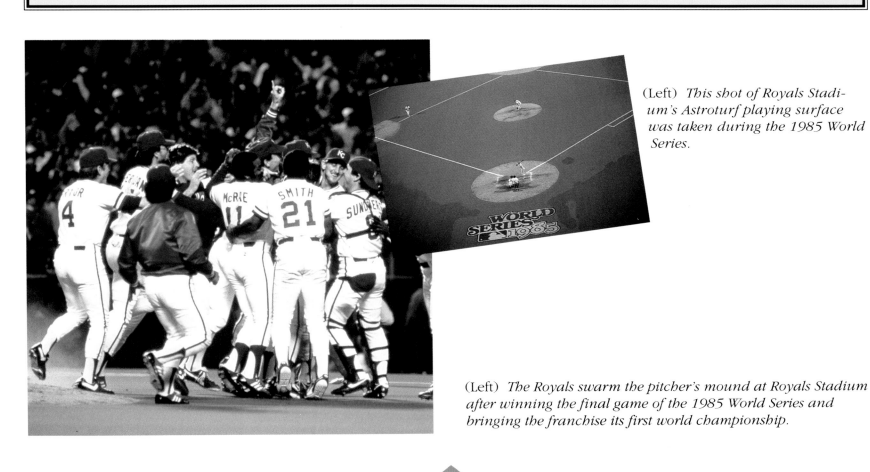

(Left) *This shot of Royals Stadium's Astroturf playing surface was taken during the 1985 World Series.*

(Left) *The Royals swarm the pitcher's mound at Royals Stadium after winning the final game of the 1985 World Series and bringing the franchise its first world championship.*

When SkyDome's retractable roof is open, most of the grand-stand and the playing surface is exposed to the Toronto sun-shine. The facility, which opened in July 1989, is the world's first stadium with a fully retractable roof.

Fans intent on seeing a game at SkyDome had better arrive early. The Blue Jays average close to 50,000 patrons per game.

SKYDOME
Toronto, Ontario

1989–

The largest McDonald's in North America can be found inside the stadium.

WHEN THE HOUSTON ASTRODOME opened in 1965, it efficiently solved a problem that had plagued baseball clubs for a century: how to play ball in bad weather. The Astrodome ensured that every game would be played in a climate-controlled environment with the temperature maintained at a comfortable 75° and with no fierce winds or distracting drizzle to affect the men on the ball field. Especially in cities where the climate is often uncomfortable for baseball—in Houston, where the Texas sun saps everyone's energy; in Seattle, where the rainy season seems to last all year; in Minneapolis, where winter arrives early and stays late—domes seem to make both economic and baseball sense.

But in solving one problem, domed stadiums created another. Watching a game under a roof prevents fans from enjoying the spring sunshine of a May day. They could never feel the balmy breezes of an August night or watch the moon rise above the right field wall. Domes drive out the bad weather, but they also keep out the good.

In the mid-1980s, when the Toronto Blue Jays and the Stadium Corporation of Ontario were planning the Jays' new home park, they were mindful of both the advantages

Toronto fans arrive at a SkyDome game in June 1991. A bit of the impressive ornamentation on the stadium's facade is visible in this photo.

Windows Restaurant, set beyond the right center field wall, provides diners with a bird's eye view of the action on the field. The Blue Jays' Fred McGriff and the Athletics' Jose Canseco have managed to smash long drives off the eatery's plexiglass windows.

Shortstop Tony Fernandez was a key player on the 1989 Blue Jays, the team that brought SkyDome its first divisional title.

and disadvantages of domed stadiums. They knew that the frigid weather in the Lake Ontario region before May and after Labor Day often made outdoor baseball a trying experience for both players and fans. What would happen, they wondered, if the Blue Jays earned a place in the World Series? How could night games be played in Toronto in mid-October? On the other hand, Canadians are outdoor people. The stadium planners knew that during the relatively short summer season, fans would prefer to watch a baseball game outdoors.

The solution was, in theory, very simple: create a sports stadium that would operate like an automobile with a convertible top, one that could be opened on splendid summer days but closed when atmospheric conditions were less than pleasing. The result—Toronto's SkyDome—was the world's first stadium with a fully retractable roof. More than a baseball field, SkyDome is one of the world's most impressive engineering feats.

With its roof closed, SkyDome looks like the Louisiana Superdome or the Houston Astrodome, a large, circular structure with a bubble-top roof and an attractively detailed facade. There are parking lots adjacent to the stadium, but automobile space has been minimized to encourage patrons to use Toronto's efficient public transportation system. Near the park are racks for hundreds of bicycles to persuade other fans to ride vehicles that neither consume gasoline nor cause serious traffic snarls.

But two or three hours before game time, weather permitting, SkyDome transforms itself into a different arena. At that time, two large roof panels begin to slide to the north end of the stadium, and a third section of the roof revolves around the perimeter of the dome and nestles snugly into place inside the other two panels, leaving the entire playing field and most of the seats exposed to the sun and sky of Toronto. The entire process—a silent and magnificent movement of steel— takes about 20 minutes. Most of the time, this engineering ballet occurs before the fans have arrived at the park, but if rain

With its roof closed, SkyDome looks like the Louisiana Superdome or the Houston Astrodome, a large, circular structure with a bubble-top roof and an attractively detailed facade.

should break out in the fifth inning, the switch is thrown to close the roof, and the patrons and players are treated to a spectacular mechanical show. The choreographer of this rooftop performance is architect Roderick Robbie, who created it in conjunction with Michael Allen, the project engineer, and a consortium of Toronto-based architecture and engineering firms.

The creators of SkyDome were also aware of another problem posed by domed stadiums: they shut off occupants from the cityscapes that surround the ballparks. The SkyDome compensates for this problem in two ways. First, the upper-deck promenade offers patrons views of the CN Tower (the world's tallest free-standing structure), Union Station, and other buildings along Toronto's skyline. Second, SkyDome's designers have brought the city into the stadium. In addition to a 54,000-seat grandstand, arranged in five decks,

(Right) When the weather is foul, SkyDome's roof is closed, and baseball in Toronto is an indoor game.

SkyDome also houses an 11-story, 348-room hotel (with 70 rooms offering a view of the field); a restaurant and bar overlooking center field; a Hard Rock Cafe behind the right field grandstand; a health club; a theater; and the largest McDonald's in North America.

Of course, the stadium's star attraction is its baseball diamond, covered with Astro-turf and set below a 33-foot-wide and 110-foot-long video display scoreboard that provides messages, high-tech graphics, and, of course, the score of the game. The playing field is symmetrical; the fences down the foul lines are 328 feet from home plate, and the center field wall is 400 feet away. In domed stadiums, however, field measurements rarely indicate whether the park favors the hitter or the pitcher. The Astrodome, which seems to have reachable outfield fences, is a pitcher's park because the ball does not carry well. On the other hand, the Hubert H. Humphrey Metrodome in Minneapolis, which is only slightly smaller than the Astrodome, has been nick-

SkyDome's walkways are enhanced by works of art that feature the signatures of the construction workers who built the stadium and artifacts unearthed during the excavation.

named "the Homer Dome" because the balls fly into the seats so frequently.

SkyDome quickly earned a reputation as a hitter's park. As soon as the Blue Jays moved in on July 5, 1989, the home runs started coming—and some of the blasts looked as if they had been shot from a cannon. Shortly after the park opened, Fred McGriff, the Jays' slugging first baseman, lined a shot off the plexiglass window of the Windows Restaurant in deep right field. In the fourth game of the 1989 American League Championship Series—the Jays won their division title in SkyDome's first season—Jose Canseco of the Oakland Athletics blasted a massive home run that landed in the fifth deck in left field, about 540 feet from home plate. The next season,

Slugger Fred McGriff is featured on the cover of this 1989 scorecard.

The 1989 American League Championship Series: SkyDome Playoffs

Toronto fans were delighted that their Blue Jays brought home a division title during the SkyDome's maiden season, edging an upstart Baltimore Oriole team in a race that was settled on the final weekend. The only problem was that the Jays would have to face the powerful Oakland A's in the American League Championship Series.

The A's were loaded with talent. Dave Stewart, Mike Moore, Bob Welch, and Dennis Eckersley anchored a pitching staff that easily led the league in earned run average, and sluggers Jose Canseco and Mark McGwire and speedster Rickey Henderson provided the staff with plenty of offensive support.

It looked bad for the Blue Jays when they lost the two opening games of the Series in Oakland by scores of 7-3 and 6-3. Back home for game three, however, the Jays rallied, despite a score of 3-0 in favor of Oakland at one point, and won 7 runs to 3. Oakland came back in game four, however, as Rickey Henderson socked two homers and Jose Canseco recorded his unforgettable 540-foot blast off of the fifth deck in left field. The final score was 6-5 in favor of the A's. The next day, Oakland ended the Blue Jays' season by beating them 4-3. The A's went on to sweep the Giants in the World Series.

Blue Jay fans were surely disappointed by the events of October 1989, but the team's roster contains enough talent to to ensure that Sky-Dome will probably be the site of future championship playoffs.

Fred McGriff slides home with a run in game three of the 1989 American League Championship Series during SkyDome's maiden season. The Blue Jays won the game by a score of 7-3 but lost the series, four games to one.

Canseco hit the restaurant overlooking center field. Undoubtedly, more tape-measure homers will follow.

Not all baseball fans would want to see a space-age stadium like SkyDome for their own home teams. Those who treasure the intimacy of Fenway Park would certainly deplore it. But in SkyDome's first full season of operation, the Blue Jays drew a record 3,885,284 fans, an average of almost 48,000 patrons per game. The stadium's creators must have done something right.

Fans pass old Comiskey Park (the white building in the background) as they enter the new stadium in a photo taken early in the 1991 season.

A Comiskey Park favorite is Carlton Fisk, who holds the American League record for homers by a catcher. His unusual uniform number, 72, is the reverse of the 27 that he wore as a Red Sox.

COMISKEY PARK
Chicago, Illinois

1991–

The new stadium's arched windows, a reminder of the old Comiskey Park, reflects the crowd entering the park.

FROM 1910 THROUGH THE END OF THE 1990 SEASON, the Chicago White Sox played baseball in Comiskey Park, making it the oldest continuously used ball field in professional sports. But age had taken its toll on the old structure—to the point where the Chisox management had begun threatening to leave Chicago and head for Florida if the state of Illinois did not build the team a new home. (The days when team owners invested their own money in a playing facility, from which they profited handsomely, have long since passed.) Governor James R. Thompson vowed to "bleed and die before I let the Sox leave Chicago." Much to the joy of area fans (many of whom come, ironically, from northern Indiana), the governor found the revenues necessary to build a new facility, and the Sox stayed in Chicago. After years of negotiations, the new stadium was built.

So on September 30, 1990, fans who attended the last game at the old park could see rising over the field the new grounds across the street. They towered over the smaller, older Comiskey. The Sox won that day behind Jack McDowell. Possibly in the name of symmetry, Mc-Dowell was named the starting pitcher on the day the new

In 1991, Frank Thomas, the Chisox first baseman in his first full year with the club, hit his team's first homer in its new stadium.

Charles Comiskey: "The Old Roman"

The man whose name adorned two White Sox ballparks was born in Chicago in 1859, the son of Irish immigrants. At age 20, he began playing semi-pro baseball, and later, in 1882, he reached the major leagues as a first baseman with the St. Louis Browns of the old American Association. As a player, Comiskey was mediocre—he averaged .264 in 13 major league seasons. His skill lay in managing, a role that he first assumed in 1883, his second season with St. Louis. From 1885 through 1888, his Browns won the American Association title. During his 12 seasons as a manager with three different clubs in three different leagues, Comiskey achieved a .608 winning percentage, the third best in major league history.

Comiskey retired as a manager after the 1894 season and immediately became a team owner, purchasing a Western League franchise in Sioux City, Iowa. He moved his team to St. Paul, Minnesota, and then, in 1901, when Ban Johnson reorganized the Western League as the American League, Comiskey brought his club to his native Chicago, naming it the White Stockings. The team won the first American League pennant. In 1910, the Old Roman erected Comiskey Park, the stadium that would host White Sox home games for the next eight decades.

Although he built winning teams, Comiskey was not popular with his players, mainly because he paid them very poorly. In 1919, his stinginess may even have helped inspire the eight poorly paid White Sox who allegedly accepted money from gamblers for losing the World Series. One of the "fixers," pitcher Ed Cicotte, had a particular money-related grudge against Comiskey, who had ordered the 29-game winner benched with two weeks left in the season because of a clause in the pitcher's contract calling for him to receive a bonus if he won 30 games. Comiskey did not live to see the White Sox win another pennant. He died in 1931 and was elected to the Baseball Hall of Fame in 1939.

The new Comiskey Park, sleek and efficient, is unlike its predecessor in many ways. In its name, however, it too pays homage to the man who founded American League baseball in Chicago.

Comiskey Park's press box is crowded with reporters.

stadium opened, April 18, 1991, and Governor Thompson threw out the ceremonial first ball.

As 44,702 fans filed in on opening day—520 more than capacity—they walked past the remains of the old stadium, which the wrecking ball had begun to attack just a few weeks earlier. Many had mixed emotions on viewing the decaying old park. One 80-year-old man returned to Chicago from Canada just to say good-bye. "Many a happy day I spent in this place," he said. "I thought it would be here forever. I'm a grown man and I almost want to cry." Even some of the younger fans lamented. "It's like destroying an antique. Seeing it put to death like this, it just makes you numb," said one. White Sox officials responded by noting that the team's glory was not in the stadium that had housed it but in the accomplishments of the greats who had played there. "The new park will create its own memories," management said.

Still, the contrast between the old and new were hard to escape on opening day. New York Times reporter Isabel Wilkerson summed up the feelings of many of the Chisox working-class fans: "If the old Comiskey was Luke Appling and Crackerjacks, a South Side Roman Colosseum, Comiskey II is grilled chicken and frozen yogurt, a factory-new Disneyland in [a] field of warehouses and bungalows." Indeed, the new Comiskey Stadium features sleek, mirrored archways and a glass-enclosed Stadium Club. There are even diapering stations in the men's rest rooms. One disgruntled fan said of the new grandeur, "It feels like going to the library."

Baseball cognoscenti are already guessing that the park will be a hitter's paradise.

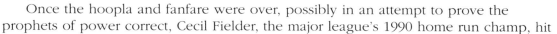

The ball seems to carry well here, and the fences are not very far from home plate. The 347 feet to the left field and right field foul poles prevent cheap shots from reaching the seats, but the 375 feet to the power alleys and the 400 feet to deepest center are not imposing.

The grass is real. Double-deck grandstands hug the area outward from behind home plate and then curve around each foul pole, where they meet single tiers of bleacher seats. These stretch across the outfield, except in straightaway center where a light-blue covering provides a solid background for hitters. Bullpens are nestled under the outfield stands, screened to prevent balls from hitting the occupants. A large scoreboard looms over the center field bleachers. The entire design of the new Comiskey Park is perfect for baseball. In fact, it was the first facility, since Royals Stadium went up in 1973, that was not designed also to serve as a football field.

Once the hoopla and fanfare were over, possibly in an attempt to prove the prophets of power correct, Cecil Fielder, the major league's 1990 home run champ, hit the first homer in the new park. Later, Rob Deer hit two, and Tony Phillips added another. Unfortunately, each of these athletes drew his salary from the Detroit Tigers. By the end of the third inning, the Sox were trailing by six runs, and some fans were heading for Indiana. The Tigers added 10 more runs in the fourth inning, making the final score 16-0. It was not an auspicious way for a team to break in its new $135-million home.

The next afternoon, the Tigers won again, but at least the Sox were able to score a run, after 24 2/3 scoreless innings, and it did take Detroit 12 innings to achieve the victory. Finally, the home team won the third game in the new park, with Frank Thomas, the first baseman playing his first full year with the Sox, hitting the team's first dinger.

In a few years, there will be a host of unforgettable moments associated with the new Comiskey Park. Undoubtedly, Mike Greenwell will poke one over the last row of the bleachers. Rickey Henderson will no doubt make a spectacular catch. And perhaps Carlton Fisk will be honored with a special day when he retires. In the meantime, baseball will be played in the new ballpark as it was played for 81 years in the old yard across the street. Pitchers will hurl, batters will swing, fans will roar, outs will be made, and runs will be scored; and they will all be set down for posterity. Thus, the prediction of a club executive, that the new park will create its own great memories, will undoubtedly come true.

(Above) *The entire design of the new Comiskey Park is perfect for baseball. In fact, it was the first facility, since Royals Stadium went up in 1973, that was not designed to also serve as a football field.*

(Right) *Old Glory guards the attractive facade of new Comiskey Park.*

(Left) *Eli Jacobs, the Orioles' owner, has a keen interest in urban design. He insisted that his team's new ballpark be integrated into the neighborhood in which it would stand.*

(Above right) *This shot of a model of the new ballpark highlights the structure's classic brick facade and arched windows, which call to mind old Comiskey Park, Fenway Park, and other ballparks of the pre-World War I era.*

The Orioles' new home field, which seats 46,000, is neatly woven into the fabric of Baltimore's Inner Harbor area.

NEW BALTIMORE STADIUM*

Baltimore, Maryland

1992–

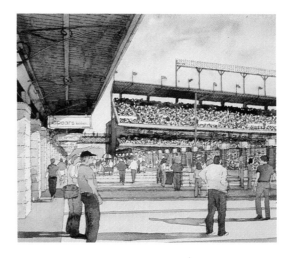

A pre-construction drawing shows fans gathering in the concourse that is set in front of the converted warehouse beyond the right field fence.

I **N 1954,** when the St. Louis Browns moved to Baltimore, they chose the name of a 19th-century American Association franchise and occupied Memorial Stadium, a new sports arena built on the ground that had once held Municipal Stadium. An unpretentious, horseshoe-shaped, uncovered, double-deck grandstand, Memorial Stadium served the Orioles well for more than 35 years and also accommodated the National Football League's Colts until that team slipped off in the night to Indianapolis in 1984. After the Colts' departure, the Maryland Stadium Authority decided to upgrade the Orioles' playing facilities so that Baltimore would not lose its baseball franchise as well. In 1988, plans were drawn for a new baseball park to be built downtown near the city's revitalized Inner Harbor area, on a piece of land that had once been occupied by Babe Ruth's father's saloon.

Opening for the 1992 season, the new park is sure to please traditional baseball fans who long for the uniqueness and intimacy of Ebbets Field, Fenway Park, Wrigley Field, and other cozy, urban ballparks. Instead of creating a 60,000-seat, symmetrical stadium in a sea of parking lots, the new park's architects, of the firm of Hellmuth, Obata &

Cal Ripken, Jr., Baltimore's franchise player, hopes that the new ballpark will inspire the team to repeat its past glories.

*Currently unnamed

Kassabaum, designed a modest, 46,000-seat arena that fits snugly into the contours of the downtown city streets. Writing in the New York Times, architecture critic Paul Goldberger called the design for the Orioles' new home "the best plan for a major-league baseball park in more than a generation."

The design was conceived essentially by Eli S. Jacobs, the Orioles' owner, and Joseph Spear, the architect in charge. Jacobs, who has a keen interest in architecture and urban design, deemed it necessary for the new Baltimore ballpark to complement the neighborhood in which it would stand. Spear, who had designed Royals Stadium in Kansas City 15 years earlier, knew that for baseball stadiums, large is not always beautiful, and he was aware that a cozy park set amid the grid of city streets could well serve fans of the National Pastime.

Just before beginning the Baltimore project, Spear had designed Pilot Field, the splendid stadium that houses the Class AAA Bisons of Buffalo, New York. Seating 19,500 patrons and expandable to 42,000 should the city be awarded a major league franchise, this cozy ballpark is wedged into the grid of downtown streets. Its steel-tube arcade and arched windows call to mind Comiskey Park, Shibe Park, and other fields of yesteryear and smartly reflect the Ellicott Square Building and other downtown Buffalo landmarks. When Pilot Field opened in 1988, it was so well received that the Bisons set a Class AAA attendance record.

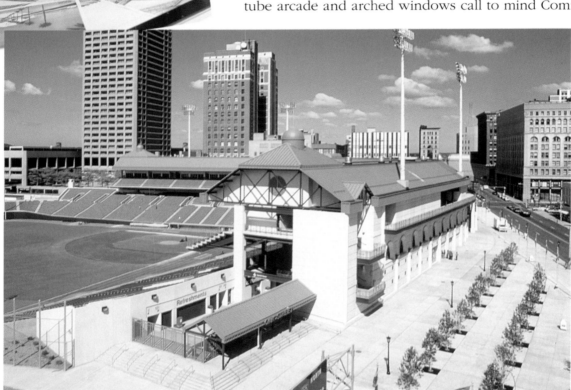

The new Baltimore stadium has been designed in the spirit of Pilot Field. Its walls are made of red brick, and its facade is bedecked with a series of arches resembling those that once adorned Comiskey Park. Its double-deck grandstand wraps around the playing field, and old-fashioned bleacher seats are set beyond the center field fence. Unlike the sloping grandstands of so many modern stadiums, the grandstand in the new Baltimore park is built tightly around the playing field in an effort to keep all of the fans close to the action on the diamond. The foul territory along the base lines is small, which will not make Orioles pitchers happy but will allow for a maximum number of fans to sit in what Red Barber would call "catbird seats."

Joseph Spear, the architect at Hellmuth, Obata & Kassabaum who designed Baltimore's new park, had previously drawn the blueprints for Royals Stadium in Kansas City and Pilot Field, a Class AAA field in Buffalo, New York. The latter can be see in the photo above.

Perhaps the most daring move in this bold "old ballpark" design, however, involves something outside the stadium. As Spear and his colleagues planned their park, they were forced to decide what to do with an 1898 brick warehouse, eight stories high and several blocks long, that sits just beyond the designated site for the right field seats. Instead of demolishing the industrial relic, the architects wisely opted to let it stand, converting it to conference space and offices to serve the team's executives. The large building splendidly complements the brick ballpark, reminding patrons that their field of green is woven into the fabric of an urban center. Inside the stadium, the grandstand provides views of the Baltimore skyline, further reminding fans that the ballpark is part of their city.

The playing field in this new park is grass, of course, and its dimensions are asymmetrical—335 feet in left field, 407 feet in deep left center, 397 feet in straightaway center, and 319 feet near the foul pole in right. (The refurbished building be-

Baltimore Memorial Stadium

Despite the excitement surrounding the opening of their new park, many Baltimoreans will mourn the loss of their old stadium. A simply designed park which, like County Stadium in Milwaukee, was built during the franchise shifts of the 1950s, Memorial Stadium played host to some great Oriole and Colt teams.

The stadium was the site of six World Series, three of which—those in 1966, 1970, and 1983—were won by the hometown Birds. On this

field, Brooks Robinson showed the world how to play third base, Jim Palmer displayed the classic windup that resulted in eight 20-victory seasons, manager Earl Weaver paced the Oriole dugout, and shortstop Cal Ripken began his long consecutive-game playing streak. On this turf, Johnny Unitas dropped long passes into the waiting arms of Raymond Berry and Lenny Moore.

(Left) *Memorial Stadium patrons will never forget Hall of Famer Jim Palmer, whose classic pitching motion led to eight 20-victory seasons.*

(Right) *From 1954 through 1991, the Orioles played their home games in Memorial Stadium.*

Moreover, the soil in the open area beyond the outfield wall was perfect for Weaver's tomato garden, and the stadium's concession stands served the best crab cakes in the world.

Old Memorial Stadium is filled with pleasant memories for Baltimore sports fans, and they are fortunate to have a replacement that should serve the city well.

yond the right field seats stands about 475 feet from home plate, a reachable target for the league's premier power hitters.) As most players will explain, however, fence measurements alone do not indicate whether this park will favor the batters or the men on the mound. The intangibles that dictate how a park "plays"—the wind currents, the density of the air, the slant of the sun's rays as they dance off the playing field—will become apparent only after several hundred innings of play, and the Baltimore fans can hardly wait for the games to commence.

Baseball traditionalists hope that this newest addition to major league play represents a new phase in stadium design, a move to the future that looks carefully back to the past. Perhaps the days of domes and plastic playing surfaces are over, and a new collection of Fenway Parks, Ebbets Fields, and Wrigley Fields will someday adorn the baseball landscape.

This overhead shot of a model of the stadium shows the old eight-story brick warehouse that will sit beyond the right field grandstand.

Acknowledgements

The producers of *The Fields of Summer* gratefully acknowledge the assistance of the following individuals in the creation of this book:

Baltimore Orioles Community Relations Department, Stephanie Kelly; Bisons Publicity Department; Boston University Special Collections, Kathy Kominis; Boston Red Sox, Debbie Matson; Brooklyn Historical Society, Clare Lamers; The Bronx County Historical Society, Laura Tosi; Chicago White Sox Public Relations, Ron Yoder; Cleveland Indians Publicity Department, John Maroon; Dwight D. Eisenhower Library, Kathleen Struss; Hellmuth, Obata & Kessabaum, Inc., Susan London; Houston Astros Publicity, Meribeth Fuqua, Rob Matwick; Houston Sports Association, Susan King; Howard University Hospital Public Relations Office, Daisy Fetts; Kansas City Royals Publicity Department, Maggie Mistler; Major League Baseball Properties, Cynthia Mc-Manus; National Baseball Hall of Fame and Museum, Inc., Pat Kelly, Dan Bennett, Steve Brauner, Sarah Kelly; New York Mets Publicity, Lynn Daley; New York Yankees Media Relations Department, Jeff Idelson, Brian Walker; Oakland A's Media Relations Department, Doreen Alvez, Kathy Jacobson; Philadelphia Phillies Public Relations Department, Christine Urban; Pittsburgh Pirates Public Relations, Sally O'Leary; University of Pittsburgh, Thomas Dunn; San Francisco Giants Print Publications Department, Mark Ray; Society of American Baseball Researchers, Robert Bluthardt; The Sporting Views, Tony Inzerillo; SkyDome Guest Services, Gail Anderson; Harry S. Truman Library, Pauline Testerman; Western Reserve Historical Society, Ann Sindelar; WGN-TV (Chicago), Joan Sorensen.

Photo Credits

t=top, b=bottom, l=left, r=right, c=center, tr=top right, tl=top left, bl=bottom left, br=bottom right, lc=left center, rc=right center

The Baltimore Orioles Publicity Dept. 157 (b), 159 (tl and tr). Photo tr is by Jerry Wachter.

The Bettmann Archive 25 (b), 32 (tr), 39 (t), 43 (b).

Boston Red Sox 2–3, 56 (t and b), 91 (b).

Alan Briere 4–5 (b), 60 (t), 65 (tr), 91 (t), 93 (b), 95 (tr and b), 122 (b), 125 (tl and br), 126 (b), 129 (b), 131 (tr and br), 133 (b).

The Brooklyn Historical Society 69 (t).

The Chicago Historical Society 30 (b), 72 (t).

Chicago White Sox Public Relations 31 (b), 34 (t), 34–35, 35 (t).

The Cincinnati Reds Publicity Office 48 (t and b), 49 (t), 51, 52 (b).

The Cleveland Indians Publicity Dept. 92.

David Forbert Photography front jacket, 85 (t), 88 (bl), 89 (b), 117 (t), 119 (br), 120 (bl).

The Historical Society of Pennsylvania 12 (t and b).

HOK Sports Facilities Corp. 152 (tl), 153 (tr), 154 (bl), 155 (tr and br), 156 (tr and b), 157 (t), 158 (t and b), 159 (b) (The photos of New Comiskey Park are by Scott McDonald, Hedrich-Blessing, © 1991. The photo of Pilot Field is by Patricia Layman Bazelon, ©1988).

The Houston Astros Public Relations Dept. 123 (t), 124 (bl), 125 (tr), 126 (bl), 127 (tr).

The Howard University Hospital Public Relations Dept. 41 (b).

Tony Inzerillo 30 (b), 72 (t), 153 (br).

Eli S. Jacobs, photo by Tom Sullivan 156 (tl).

The Kansas City Royals 96–97, 140 (t and b), 141 (t and b), 143 (t), 144 (l and r), 145 (t, bl, and r).

Library of Congress 62 (b).

John Maley 54 (t), 55 (t), 59 (t).

National Baseball Library, Cooperstown, New York 13 (t and b), 14, 14–15, 15, 17, 20 (b), 22 (bl), 24 (tl, r), 26 (b), 32 (tl), 32 (b), 33 (t), 37 (t), 39 (b), 40, 42, 44, 52 (t), 53 (tr), 55 (b), 57 (t), 58 (b), 61 (b), 65 (rc, rb), 70 (t and b), 71 (b), 73 (t), 74 (bl and r), 75 (b), 76 (tl and b), 77 (bl), 78 (t), 80, 81 (t and b), 83, 84 (bl and r), 94 (tl, tr, and br), 95 (l), 102 (bl), 103 (b), 104 (tr), 108 (b), 110 (t), 114 (b), 115 (br), 118 (t), 121 (b), 124 (tl), 126 (tl), 127 (br), 131 (rc), 132 (tl and bl), 134 (tl and r), 136 (tl), 138 (bl), 143 (bl and r), 150 (b).

National Park Service—Abbie Rowe, Courtesy Harry S Truman Library 36 (t).

The New York Yankees 76 (r), 85 (b), 86 (t), 88 (r).

The Philadelphia Phillies Publicity Dept. 17.

Pittsburgh Pirates Publicity 18 (t and b), 19 (t and b), 20 (t), 21 (b), 22 (tl), 23 (t).

Lynn Radeka 105 (t and b), 109 (r), 111 (b), 112 (bl), 113 (t), 135 (t), 136 (tr), 137 (b), 138 (t), 139 (t).

The New York Mets Public Relations Dept. 118 (b), 118–119, 119 (tr), 120 (br), 121 (t).

The San Francisco Giants/Martha Jane Stanton, photographer 104 (tl), 160.

David Scott 146 (b), 147 (t and b), 148 (t), 149 (t and b), 150 (t).

SkyDome Guest Services 146 (t).

The Sporting News, Rich Filling 29.

SuperStock Inc. 89 (t), 119 (l).

The University of Pittsburgh, Dept. of University Relations/Jim Burke 23 (bl and r).

UPI/Bettmann 6, 7, 8, 9, 16, 17, 22 (tr), 22 (br), 24 (b), 25 (t), 26 (t), 27 (t), 28 (t), 28–29, 30 (tr), 33 (b), 36 (b), 37 (b), 38 (t and b), 41 (t), 43 (t), 44–45, 45, 46, 47 (t and b), 49 (b), 50, 53 (l, br), 54 (b), 57 (b), 58 (t), 59 (b), 60 (b), 62 (t), 63, 64 (t and b), 65 (l), 66, 67 (t and b), 68 (t), 69 (b), 70–71, 71 (t), 72 (b), 74 (tl), 77 (br), 78 (b), 79 (t and b), 82–83, 84 (t), 86 (b), 87 (t and b), 90 (t), 92–93, 94 (t), 94 (bl), 98, 99 (t and b), 100 (t and b), 101 (t and b), 102 (t and br), 103 (t), 104 (b), 111 (t), 112 (tl and r), 113 (b), 114 (t), 115 (t and bl), 116, 117 (b), 120 (t), 122 (t), 123 (b), 124 (tr), 127 (l), 128, 129 (t), 130 (l and r), 131 (l), 132 (r), 133 (t), 134 (b), 135 (b), 136 (b), 137 (t), 138 (br), 139 (b), 142, 148 (b), 151, 152 (br), 154 (tl).

Western Reserve Historical Society 90 (b).

WGN-TV, photo by Steve Green 77 (t).

The William Wrigley, Jr. Company 73 (b).

The baseball team trademarks appearing in this book were reproduced with permission from Major League Baseball Properties, Inc.